VIVA MEXICO!

BY MARCUS DALRYMPLE

Marcus Dalrymple was born in Buenos Aires, Argentina in 1966. He was educated in Mexico and at boarding school in England. Marcus trained as a journalist before becoming an English teacher. He is married to Sharon and they live with their three sons in North Yorkshire. **'Viva Mexico!'** is his first book.

Note to the reader: each chapter begins with a short vignette alluding to when the author was growing up in Mexico in the 1970's

VIVA MEXICO!

Black Cat Publications
Originally published in the U.S.A by Black Cat Books
an imprint of Black Cat Publications

Copyright Marcus Dalrymple 2011
Maps and illustrations Marcus Dalrymple 2011
All Rights Reserved.

The right of Marcus Dalrymple to be identified as the author of this work has been asserted in accordance with sections 77 and 78 of the Copyright Designs and Patents Act 1988

This book is sold subject to the condition that it shall not, by way of trade or otherwise, be lent, re-sold, hired out or otherwise circulated in any form of binding or cover other than that in which it is published and without a similar condition including this condition being imposed on the subsequent purchaser

Black Cat Publications
Printed by CreateSpace

Note to the reader: in an effort to safeguard the privacy of several individuals, the author has changed their names, and in some cases disguised identifying characteristics or used composite characters.

ISBN-10 1460943937
EAN-13 9781460943939

BIBLIOGRAPHY

1. **The Conquest of New Spain**. Bernal Diaz. Translated by J.M Cohen 1963. Penguin Books
2. ***Virginibus Puerisque.*** *Robert Louis Stephenson 1881*
3. **Terry's Guide to Mexico.** Boston and New York, Houghton Mifflin Co.; [etc.] 1923.

Front cover photograph: *'Tierra Caliente'* by Marcus Dalrymple.

CONTENTS

Chapter 1 – La Llegada 1
Chapter 2 – Valle por Monumento 11
Chapter 3 – El Mercado 15
Chapter 4 – La Escuela 23
Chapter 5 – Viva Mexico 33
Chapter 6 – El Distrito Federal 43
Chapter 7 – El Cine 55
Chapter 8 – Una Vista 61
Chapter 9 – La Tertulia 67
Chapter 10 – La Matanza de Tlatelolco 79
Chapter 11 – Las Lluvias 85
Chapter 12 – El Almuerzo 93
Chapter 13 – El Vagabundo 105
Chapter 14 – La Comida 117
Chapter 15 – La Cantina 133
Chapter 16 – El Dia de los Muertos 141
Chapter 17 – Las Mariposas 151
Chapter 18 – Hacia las Montañas 161
Chapter 19 – El Campamento 173
Chapter 20 – La Venganza 183
Chapter 21 – La Cocina Mexicana 195
Chapter 22 – Curas 205
Chapter 23 – La Posada 211
Chapter 24 – Una Carta 227
Chapter 25 – Taxis y Taxistas 235

Chapter 26 – La Casa de los Espiritus. 249
Chapter 27 – Picaruelos 255
Chapter 28 – Historia 263
Chapter 29 – El Mal de Ojo 271
Chapter 30 – La Vida Loca 283
Chapter 31 – A Zihuatanejo 293
Chapter 32 – La muerte de Lupita Guadarama . . . 317
Chapter 33 – El Pinche Gringo 327
Chapter 34 – Popocatepetl. 335
Chapter 35 – Abejas 345
Chapter 36 – El Triathlon 355
Chapter 37 – La Carretera. 365
Chapter 38 – La Copa Mundial. 377
Chapter 39 – Amigos y Conocidos 383
Chapter 40 – Perros salvajes. 395
Chapter 41 – A Chiapas 401

Epilogue – Crusando Mexico 419
Glossary. 431
Acknowledgements. 447

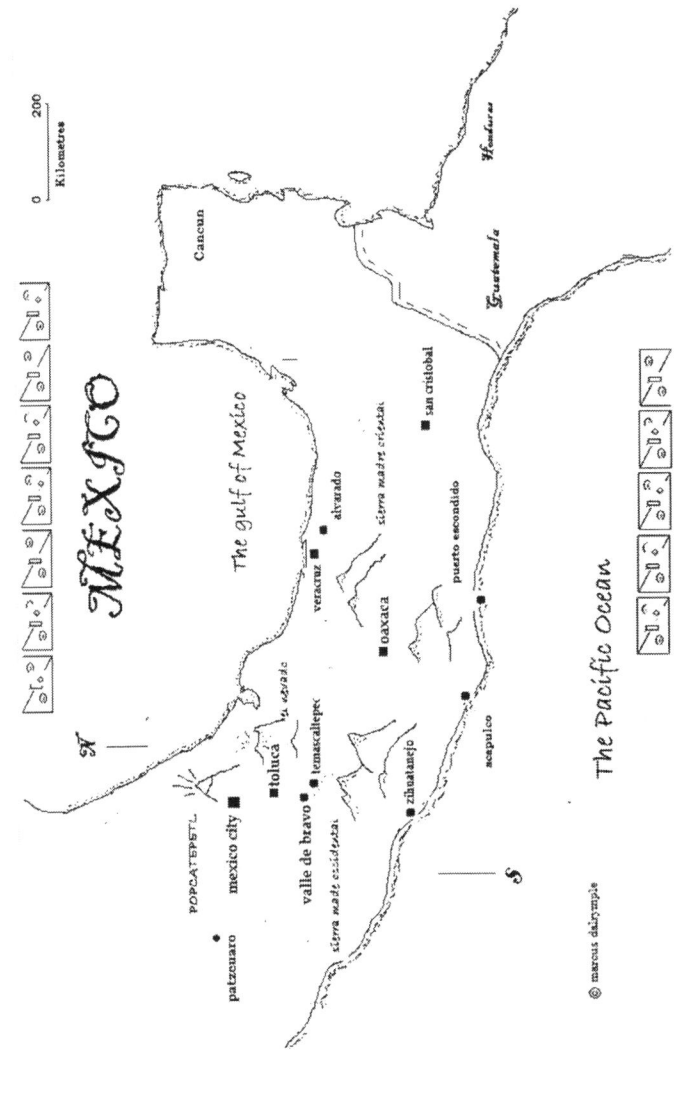

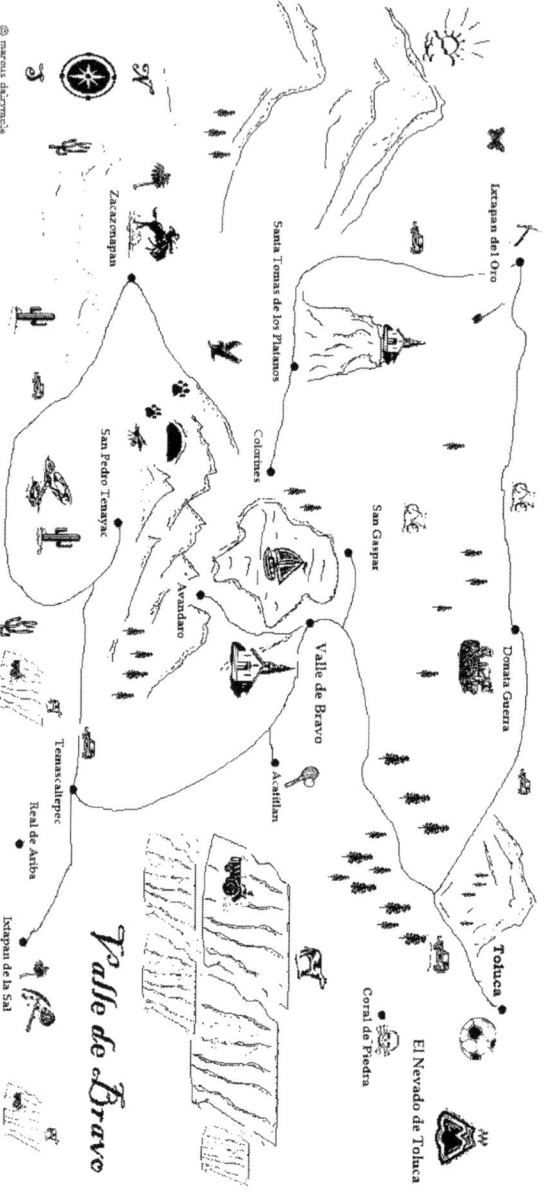

CHAPTER 1

LA LLEGADA

Outside there is a *Jacaranda* tree and a big imposing wooden gate. The house is large, modern and spacious with a cold marbled floor and wooden bookcases. A swinging door leads to the breakfast room. There are posters; I remember one with portraits and details of the kings and queens of England. The playroom is enormous with a red carpet and a metal rocking horse on springs and an old mattress on the floor. I remember a garden with a wooden swing and a green Wendy house. There is a big fireplace with an adjacent cupboard for storing wood and a room in the basement with a huge boiler and gas cylinders.

***

The night I arrived back in *Valle de Bravo*, there had been a tropical rainstorm that brought the power lines down and plunged the town into darkness. As we drove up cobbled *Pagaza* Street, shadowy, spectral figures clad in *rebozos* and *ponchos* hurried from doorway to doorway to escape the torrent of water running off the rooftops. And then the storm ceased, as suddenly as it had descended and getting out of the car a familiar scent greeted me: it was the perfume of fresh air, bougainvillea and pine woods.

My first day back in Valle began with an invitation to breakfast at the Blackmores. We sat on their terrace overlooking the lake, pine clad hills rolling away into the distance. Apart from a few more houses on the edge of the lake and a few less trees on the horizon, the view from their house was exactly as I remembered it.

Early morning is the best time of day in Valle. The sky is always blue and cloudless and the lake is as still and smooth as a pane of green glass. From the Blackmore's terrace, perched half way up the hill behind Valle, we watched the town gradually waking up. First, a single fisherman ventured out onto the lake, his oars gently dipping into the syrupy water. Then the gasman, selling cylinders from a decrepit lorry rumbled down the street. His assistant, bare to the waist, spanners dangling from

LA LLEGADA

his belt, hung precariously out of the back shouting '*Gas,*' repeatedly as the truck made its way from one end of town to the other. Church bells tolled and uniformed children scurried in all directions to catch buses and taxis to school.

From the house looking south towards the parish of *Santa María*, women weighed down with baskets of fresh bread emerged from the bakers. By now it was 10 o'clock and other fishermen, some in motorboats were on the lake. Traffic noises increased and more voices were heard floating over the rooftops: '*Vendo leña,*' – 'Wood for sale!' shouted someone. '*Agua, agua,*' called another.

On leisurely mornings at the Blackmores, breakfast was a three course affair. First there was papaya with freshly squeezed lime juice and rough cane sugar. This was followed by cereal and then fried free range eggs with bright orange yolks, crispy, salty bacon, sweet tomatoes and chilli sauce and hot strong coffee from *Veracruz*. If you were still hungry after that, there were freshly baked rolls and Nancy's homemade marmalade.

Everyone in Valle knew Nancy and Robert Blackmore. They were part of its history. More than the pillars of the British community, they were its cornerstone. In the context of Valle, the Blackmores were both unique and typical. Unique because no one else possessed their patrician charm and restrained English taste. They were also typical because, like the few other British residents, they moved to Valle having owned a weekend house in the village to escape the pollution of Mexico City and to lead the life of their choice.

Their house was a rambling bungalow with wooden beams and fireplaces in every room. It was the kind of house that children loved. Their front gate was a small green door set in a high stone wall on *El Pino* Street. A set of steps climbed through a jungle of vegetation, passed a fishpond to their terrace. The house was full of surprises. A passageway from the terrace led to a hideaway bunkhouse for their grandchildren and another to Nancy's studio. Their sitting room and study were little corners of England tucked away in the middle of Mexico. There were old family portraits and a comfortable floral patterned three piece suite. A travelling chest stood against one wall and a collection of coffee table books on art and photography were stacked on a table.

The study would not have been out of place in rural Yorkshire. The room smelt faintly of wood smoke, pipe tobacco and old books and on the desk were sepia photographs of Robert's old regiment.

Out the back in the small garden stood a lime tree that showered Nancy and Robert with baskets of fruit every year. There were also three other little surprises: a small plunge pool and two guest bedrooms, one of which was my accommodation during my first days back in Valle where I found a large black scorpion on an old edition of Robert Louis Stevenson's novel 'Treasure Island.'

***

The school provided me with a house and after two days it was ready for me to move into. It was situated in the appropriately named *Calle de la Culebra* – Snake Street – not because there were more snakes there than anywhere else, but because it wound its way in serpentine fashion from the square to the top of the hill behind Valle. My house, number 101, was about a third of the way up.

The outside gave very little away. Like most houses in Valle, there was just a brown wooden gate set into a white washed *adobe* wall which was partially covered in an anarchic honeysuckle. The gate opened into a small stone paved yard with an orange tree. A black wrought iron fence separated my house from my neighbour and landlady, *Doña Josefina*. There was room in the yard for a pile of firewood and two gas cylinders. Three large windows looked into the kitchen.

I opened the front door to find the late afternoon sun streaming into the sitting room. From the front door, two steps descended into the spacious kitchen furnished with a heavy wooden table and four chairs. Another set of steps led to the sitting room. Here there was a huge open fireplace, a coffee table and a comfortable sofa and armchairs. A flight of stairs rose to the first floor with two bedrooms and a beautiful tiled bathroom with a ceramic basin. The larger of the two rooms had a cosy brick fireplace and huge window with a panoramic view of the lake and hills beyond. I liked the polished, knotted floorboards and the heavy wardrobe. The house smelt damp and dusty. The water heater, a Heath Robinson contraption, was rusty and out of order with bare wires protruding

LA LLEGADA

from unlikely places. There were cobwebs everywhere and in one, a hapless scorpion struggled desperately but the 'piece de resistance' was the the roof terrace leading off a third attic bedroom and a spiral staircase with a view of the whole of Valle.

After exploring every cupboard and alcove, I unpacked my suitcase. I had brought very little with me from England: a few personal effects, clothing and one or two favourite books. I had assumed I could buy everything else locally, so unpacking didn't take very long. By now it was early evening, the lake was still again and the sun had begun its descent behind distant hills. I went downstairs and sat in the airy sitting room. I felt suddenly excited about being back in Mexico after an absence of 17 years. I wanted to rush out and explore the town and return to streets and squares that I remembered as a child. Was the old, blind sweet seller who used to sit on the corner of *Calle de la Revolución* still there? I wondered if I could locate some of the houses we had rented as a family all those years ago but I didn't know where to begin and in the end I went upstairs and lay on the bed and felt the cool, crisp sheets beneath me. I closed my eyes and listened to the sounds outside.

A woman called to her young son, I heard distant shouting, a dog barking and the occasional car rumbling down the hill and then I fell asleep.

***

When I awoke, it was dark. Stepping outside I found that it had rained. Rivulets of muddy water flowed over the cobblestones and the roof tiles glistened under the street lamps. I walked to the centre of town – to the square lined with benches and trees and a bandstand in the middle. It was Sunday night and mass in the Church of *San Francisco* had just ended. The *zocalo* and surrounding streets were full of Sunday strollers out for a *paseo*. I bought a lemon *paleta* and sat on one of the few empty benches. Small children in their Sunday best kicked plastic footballs. Two overweight men sitting opposite me wearing straw hats and chewing toothpicks patted their bellies, laughed and stretched their legs revealing knee length cowboy boots with steel toe caps. A trio of old widows dressed in black linked arms and gossiped in hushed tones as they circumnavigated the square. *Mazahua* women, their barefoot children dressed in brightly coloured petticoats sat on rush mats on the ground selling embroidered blankets, tablecloths and purses.

I observed a curious procession before me. A circle of giggling girls walked in a clockwise direction around the square and encircling them, moving in the opposite direction was a group of young men. They flirted, exchanged furtive glances, some pretending to ignore each other but as darkness fell and the balloon sellers, taco vendors and shoe shine boys began to drift home, couples formed and wandered off, boy leading girl to secluded spots in darkened streets. I wondered what privacy these young couples had in a town where houses were small and cramped and families were often large and extended. On many nights I would return up semi lit Culebra to find the same couple sitting on my neighbour's doorstep touching and whispering.

CHAPTER 2

VALLE POR MONUMENTO

I'm sitting on the green rug in the hall aged two. My eyes begin to sting and burn. Then my fingers turn a hot red. I am crying and my face feels puffy. Mum rushes in from the kitchen. She has no idea what has happened. I've touched a *Jalapeño* chilli.

***

If you drive west out off Mexico City along *Avenida de Toluca* you quickly find yourself in the foot hills of the *Sierra Madre Occidental*. An hour later, having passed *El Desierto de los Leones* on your left, you begin climbing towards Toluca, which at 8,500 feet above sea level is Mexico's highest and sixth largest city.

Toluca sprawls across an enormous plain and lies in the shadows of *Xinantecatl*, the fourth highest volcano in the country which rises to over

15 thousand feet. Toluca is reputedly the coldest city in Mexico and is often shrouded in mist. Dusty football pitches, herds of scrawny sheep, highways and gloomy outskirts compete for space in this sparse upland wasteland. There is little to recommend the city except its fruit and vegetable market and its football team but a 20 minute drive along a straight road takes you beyond the city's suburbs and into the forested slopes of the *sierra*.

The road twists and turns through pine and deciduous woods with occasional glimpses of Mazahua settlements. After an hour and a half, the forest ahead opens up dramatically to reveal a view of Valle de Bravo's huge lake a thousand feet below, the town itself still obscured by hills. And then as if no time at all has passed, you are driving through a large pink archway that spans the road which welcomes visitors with the words, '*Bienvenidos al antiguo pueblo de Valle de Bravo.*'

Here tarmac gives way to ancient cobbles; and white washed houses with balconies crowded with geraniums and neat wooden gates greet

VALLE POR MONUMENTO

you. There are restaurants, hotels and shops and the clear, clean mountain air is the perfect antidote for the clogging fumes of the capital.

CHAPTER 3

EL MERCADO

There's a knock at the door. It's past midnight. A light comes on in the hall, its thin illumination under the door. I can hear whispered conversation in Spanish and a woman crying. It's morning. A dog barks in the distance and a cock crows. A man was killed last night, stabbed in a fight. Another is on the run. His wife came knocking on our door and pleaded with dad to help her husband escape from the *Federales*.

***

On my first Saturday in Valle I went shopping. All there was in the stale smelling refrigerator was half a can of coke and some mouldy apples left by the previous tenant. The covered market was situated in the centre of town off *Juarez Street* named after Mexico's first *indigena* president, *Benito Juarez*. I remembered as a child recoiling at the squalor of the market, but in recent times, new hygiene regulations had transformed the place and there were now toilets in the corner where previously shoppers and vendors would have squatted to relieve themselves.

It was a thronging mass of colour and variety. There were *piñatas* hanging from the ceiling and stalls piled high with every imaginable fruit and vegetable, herb and spice: mangoes, avocados, guavas, passion fruit, green, red and yellow chillies, pineapples, papayas, melons of various varieties and bananas of every shape length and size. There were beans and vivid purple lettuces, mushrooms and other fungi and piles of fresh coriander, parsley, basil and wormwood. I brought a brightly coloured string bag and stopped by a large, merry faced *marchante* who was standing behind a mountain of blackberries and buckets of tomatoes, carrots and courgettes.

'What would you like *gringo*?' she shouted above the din, revealing a mouthful of gold fillings.

'I have everything you desire,' she said winking at me. I picked out a selection of fruit and vegetables which she weighed for me scribbling the cost down on the corner of a newspaper.

'That will be 18 pesos,' she declared before adding, 'I am an honest woman you know, when you come to the market again come to me, come to *Lupita*,' and she laughed.

I left Lupita and wandered around the other stalls. There were stands selling honeycomb and sticky sweets covered in flies. I stopped at a herbalist selling wood chips, dried flowers and roots and teas to cure kidney failure, fatigue, and loss of weight, high blood pressure, depression and infertility. There was something both beautiful and grotesque about the market and its mixture of sights and smells. Among the fragrant marigolds and ripe, juicy fruit there were children begging and wiping flies from their eyes, and an old man with two amputated legs sat on a piece of sackcloth on the cold hard floor. Despite the fluorescent strip lighting and efforts to clean up the market, I felt as if I had stepped back in time to a place far removed from the modern supermarkets of my home with their neat rows of cellophane wrapped foodstuffs and vacuum packed, pre-cooked dinners.

I lugged my shopping back through the centre of town. Being a weekend, there was more traffic and activity in the streets than usual. Nut sellers and florists had set up stands along the crowded pavements and there were more beggars and stray dogs than on weekdays. Young, nervous policemen clutching machine guns stood on street corners. The shoe shine boys were doing a brisk trade with queues of customers lining up at their booths.

From the square, I walked down Pagaza Street. The basket seller on the corner had piled up his wares outside his shop hoping to attract the steady flow of pedestrians passing by. The barbershop was full with old men talking politics and football and beneath the colonnades the taco vendors were busy fanning charcoal fires and feeding eager clients. I was tempted to stop, so delicious was the smell of roasting tortillas, shredded chicken and tomato sauce, but I wanted to get my shopping home.

I turned off Pagaza and headed up steep *San Sebastian* Street with its white washed houses and balconies crowded with Busy Lizzies. As I was walking towards Culebra, I met a boy coming down the street with three donkeys laden with firewood. He stopped and asked me if I needed any. We negotiated the price of a donkey load and I paid him 25 pesos. He followed me back to the house and unloaded the stack of wood into my yard. We got talking.

'What is your name?' I asked him.

'My name is *Joaquin, Señor* I am 10 years old.'

'Do you go to school as well as work?'

'Of course Señor, after working for my father in the mornings I attend afternoon classes at the *Morelos* primary school.'

'Do you live in Valle?' I felt I was being intrusive, but I was intrigued by this friendly boy who seemed equally eager to speak to a gringo.

'No Señor. I live many leagues away on a *ranchito* in the hills. My family has a little small holding with a few chickens and a field of maize.'

I admired his keen business sense. He was a genuine little hustler. When he had finished stacking my wood, he jumped on his donkey.

'I must go Señor, I still have these two donkey loads to sell before nightfall, but I am at your service any time you need wood or *ocote*.'

***

By now it was one o'clock and I was hungry. I decided to go out and explore the town. Locking my wooden gate, I strolled out towards the market again. Earlier in the day I had spotted the food stalls, between the butchers and the greengrocers. Here there were separate kitchens each with their own tables and benches serving different specialities. I stopped at a sign that read '*Tonio's*.' It bore a cartoon of a chef with a drooping moustache holding a frying pan. There was a spare place at the end of a busy table, so I sat down and studied the menu which was chalked up on a blackboard above the stove. Presently Tonio appeared to take my order. He was rotund with cropped black hair and a fleshy boyish complexion. Apart from the white apron around his waist he looked nothing like the cartoon chef.

'Are you Yankee?' he asked me in broken English, grinning. Tonio had an effeminate manner of speaking.

'No I'm English,' I replied.

'Ah di Inglis, I love di Inglis. Di Yankees no appreciate good food. I work San Francisco one tine. Beautiful boys but di food was terrible. So wataya want?' he asked, changing the subject abruptly.

I ordered mushroom soup and *enchiladas*. He winked at me.

'In one moment,' he said and scurried back to his stove.

Tonio had two Mazahua girls working as waitresses but he did all the cooking.

'Why don't you set up a restaurant?' I asked him when he returned with my food.

'I dona need for restaurant. I need pay too much.' He said rubbing his fingers together

'Here in di market I pay 300 pesos a year, I cook what I want; and look at all di people! They love Toni, Toni is di best,' and with that he raised his outstretched hand to his lips and blew a salutary kiss to us all.

The food was certainly good and the helpings were generous and accompanied by a basket of tortillas and green chilli and tomato sauce. Tonio took a break from his work and joined me.

'I like practise my Inglis. How d'ya like di good looking Mexican boys?' He asked winking at me again.

'What do you mean?' I pretended not to understand.

'I mean do you like to take di Mexican boys or di beautiful Mexican girls?' And he shrieked with laughter and then apologised.

'You see my friend, I am what Mexican calls *maricon* – homosexual, but dona worry, I am just di cook and good friend to you.'

CHAPTER 4
LA ESCUELA

I'm five years old and in love with Maria Freitag. She's 15 and has a heart shaped patch on her jeans. Maria rides like a cowgirl and can do flips and somersaults on the trampoline. Her father, *Guillermo* owns the fastest boat on the lake. But Maria is off to boarding school and has a boyfriend called *Luis Echeverría.*

***

La Escuela Valle de Bravo began with four children and their mothers in 1990. The school room was a sitting room; the playground, the garden, but by the time I joined the staff, it occupied a four acre site and offered a bilingual education to more than 100 pupils from nursery through to secondary.

The headmistress was *Alejandra Gerrard*. She was the granddaughter of *Plutarco Calles*; a

Mexican dictator whose face still adorned the 100 *peso* note. In the 1930's he persecuted the clergy and closed the churches. It was a bleak, bloody period in an already turbulent history and one which Graham Greene recorded in his Mexican journal 'The Lawless Roads.'

After a week's holiday spent settling into my new surroundings, I cycled up to the school for the first staff meeting of the term. The route took me up a steep hill behind my house and through the poorest neighbourhood of Valle where children ran about barefoot and emaciated dogs scavenged for scraps among the rotting rubbish. This was the forgotten community of Valle living in tumbledown shacks without running water or electricity. But there was a friendly reception for me as I cycled past.

'*Hola guerro,*' shouted a couple of old women from their doorways.

Huddled on the hillside were four converted stables made of painted adobe with terracotta tiled roofs, centred on a large courtyard with a fountain. A sign at the gate read 'La Escuela Valle de Bravo.' There was a small football pitch, a basketball court and a climbing frame. A barn had been transformed into an open air art room with storage for paper and materials.

It was at the school that I met Mark Carter. He was tall and slim with dark brown hair and moustache. Had he been wearing a *sombrero* he would have resembled a Mexican bandit. Mark had been in Mexico three years. Originally from Rotherham, he had trained as a design and technology teacher and applied for jobs abroad. A stint in the Bahamas had led to jobs in the U.S and eventually he had drifted down to Mexico where he had found work at the Edron, one of the British schools in Mexico City. He had been in Valle a year.

When staff meetings were over and everyone had prepared their classrooms for the first day of term, Mark invited me to lunch. He lived on an avocado plantation in a log cabin below the school. Four, flea invested mangy dogs sat on his porch all day and enjoyed the scraps from his table. In the dry season his garden was showered with avocados. In the rainy season his cabin became a haven for scorpions. They rested black and silent on the walls and scurried into dark corners when he opened his front door. He made me a hamburger and a cup of Orange Pekoe tea and we sat with the dogs outside watching the rain clouds blowing in from the south and listening to the first rumble of thunder. Mark briefed me about the school, describing a typical day, the children, the staff and some of the more difficult, eccentric parents. There was *Omayam*, the son of a celebrated Mexican photographer who lived out on a dusty ranch and came into school on an improvised cart made from old tyres and pulled by a horse. 'His parents are divorced,' Mark explained. 'His father exhibits all over Mexico and his mother is a mad herbalist. Omayam is often left to look after himself. He's a bit wild!'

'The parents,' he continued, 'are a mixture of local families, entrepreneurs and people who have moved out of Mexico City for a better life. Often dad works in the City and comes down at weekends and mum is left here all week with the kids and spends her time at the country club or shopping. Some of the children are very indulged. The nicest kids come from local families who have had to make big financial sacrifices to send their children here.'

By now it was pouring and we moved inside. Mark lit a fire and we continued talking.

'There are families like the *Porteros*. The father used to beat up the mother so they escaped here to Valle from Mexico City. Alejandra thinks they will be leaving soon because the father has tracked them down and has threatened to kill them all!'

Mark and I were the only foreign teachers at the school. The rest were all Mexicans, most of them natives of Valle.

Mark rented his cabin from Mochis. With his lean build, craggy face and steely grey hair and moustache, he bore a remarkable resemblance to James Coburn. Mochis was born to Lithuanian parents who had escaped to Mexico in the early 1940's from the Holocaust. Mochis had been brought up on a rustic farm outside Valle. He had had no formal education. Instead he had been left in the capable hands of a *meztizo*, who had taught Mochis everything there was to know about the local flora and fauna and how to survive in the mountains with no more than a *machete*.

Mochis was one of Valle's many eccentrics. He lived in a tumbledown shack next to Mark's cabin and owned land in and around Valle. Before he retired, he worked as a free lance for various pharmaceutical companies travelling the republic in a 60's Volkswagen van collecting snake venom.

'He was an expert at catching rattlesnakes,' Mark told me. 'He used to catch them by hand from the back of the neck. Mark went on to describe Mochis' arms.

'You can see where he's been bitten; he's got livid red scars all the way up his arms and he's missing two fingers tips!'

Mochis was a survivor. When he was in his early 20's he set himself the challenge of living homeless on the streets of San Francisco.

'He wanted to see if he could get by in an urban jungle in the same way that he could out in the bush,' Mark explained.

During the first weeks of his experiment he slept rough with other down and outs in cardboard boxes underneath the Golden Gate Bridge. He ate food scraps left in bins and waste from bakeries and fast food joints. But before long he had earned himself several nights in cheap hotels and some good hot meals.

His first find of any value was a gold ring which he spotted amongst some rubbish in the gutter. He took it to a pawn shop and traded it in for $100. Soon he was finding other things. He found a wallet full of cash under a bench at the central train station and clothes that had been thrown out that were perfectly decent once he had washed them. He found watches, cufflinks, coins and bracelets.

'During his six months in San Francisco, Mochis told me that he only had to sleep rough on the streets a handful of times.' Mark clearly admired Mochis but described him as 'Tight as a gnat's backside' when it came to spending money maintaining his cabins.

Just a month before my arrival, Mark almost blew his head off when his water heater exploded.

'I went to ignite it after replacing a gas cylinder, but the valve regulating the flow of gas had worn thin and when I lit the match, a ball of flame shot out of the flue. It singed my eye lids and eyebrows and burnt my forehead.'

Fortunately, Mark's girlfriend Lesley who was a doctor was staying and was able to administer First Aid.

'My eyelids were stuck together for several days and my face felt as if the whole thing was about to peel off. Mochis was very unsympathetic and refused to fix the heater until I threatened to sue him,' Mark laughed and put the kettle on for another cup of tea.

I asked him about Lesley – her name sounded so English.

'No she's from a large family from Yucatan. Her father is a retired school caretaker. Lesley works in forensics in a clinic in Mexico City for victims of rape. It's pretty grizzly work because the convictions for rape in Mexico are few and far between. The police generally take the view that rape victims are largely responsible for what has happened to them so Lesley's work is often frustrating and ultimately futile.'

I asked Mark how he spent his free time and discovered that he enjoyed playing pool. I had never really played, but in exchange for some regular games I persuaded him to take up mountain biking and to accompany me on local rides exploring the hills and valleys around Valle. The following day he bought a bike and we played our first game of pool in a shabby cantina off Culebra. I lost all six frames but learned a trick or two!

༄

CHAPTER 5

VIVA MEXICO!

Tomorrow we return to Mexico City. That means mum will give us a peso each to buy sweets from the old blind man who sits on the corner. His mouth is full of gold fillings. I'll buy sticky tamarind, peanut paste, packets of sugary, salty chilli powder, banana flavoured *chicles* and cinnamon sweets.

***

Shortly after my arrival in Valle, the town celebrated Independence Day, the biggest national festival which is celebrated annually on the 15th and 16th of September.

In villages, towns and cities throughout the republic the fiesta recalls the memorable moment during the early hours of the 16th September 1810, when *Hidalgo de Costilla* (popularly known as the Father of Mexico) rang the bells of his parish church and summoning together his congregation of *Dolores Queretaro*, he raised the cry of freedom and independence from Spain which is remembered and re-enacted in El Grito!

'Will you be free?' he thundered. 'Will you recover the lands stolen from your forefathers by the hated Spanish more than 300 years ago? If so, we must act now. *Viva Mexico! Viva la independencia*!'

During the Spanish occupation, society was made up of four distinct classes or castes: the *gachupines, creoles, meztizos* and *indios*. The indios were looked upon by the Spanish as an inferior race. It took a strong stand by the Roman Catholic Church to convince society that they too had souls to save. In the community they were viewed as little more than slaves, working in mines and on farms where they were treated not much better than animals.

The meztizos, a mixture of *indio* and Spanish blood, could hold menial jobs in government and private enterprise but all the important political positions and church offices were held by Spanish born gachupines. The creoles, of Spanish parents but born in Mexico, were able to hold lesser salaried posts and own property.

Instead of fostering small independent farms as occurred in the New England colonies, New Spain was divided into huge *encomiendas*. The owner, or *encomedero*, often an absentee landlord, was entitled to the labour of all the indios on his land and to absolute rule. To counter the greed and ruthlessness of the lay colonists, the Roman Catholic kings of Spain sent out groups of friars; first Franciscans, Dominicans and Augustinians and finally Jesuits who soon won the affection and admiration of the indios whom they defended vigorously. The Church recognised the religious needs of the indios, offered them an acceptable theology and more importantly, a role in the communion of men. Without the Church, the Mexicanos (the new race of meztizos) might never have thrived at all. Towards the end of Spanish rule the meztizos had grown by 1800 to some two million. Many had obtained education and some wealth and they had become restless. Although an internal explosion had become inevitable, it took violent changes outside Mexico to precipitate a shifting of class forces within.

The French Revolution, the rise of Napoleon and the collapse of the Spanish monarchy were the levers that tipped Mexico into its War of Independence. When Napoleon installed his brother Joseph on the Spanish throne, the Spanish people refused to recognise him. In Mexico, the Municipal Government of Mexico City submitted a plan to the viceroy to the effect that Mexico should govern itself until a Spanish king could occupy the throne. The Gachupines, fearful of losing control of the colonial government, seized the viceroy and imprisoned him. The independence movement was crushed temporarily.

In 1810, in the towns of Queretaro, San Miguel and Dolores, an area now known as the Cradle of Independence, a group of conspirators, among them Father Hidalgo de Costilla, began meeting under the pretext of literary studies. Others in the group included Miguel Dominguez, the mayor of Queretaro, Ignacio Allende and Igancio Aldama, both disenchanted officers in the King's regiment. Together they planned to start a revolt on October first 1810, but informants betrayed their plans to the authorities. The mayor's wife, Doña Josefina Dominguez, was aware that her husband had been betrayed and warned the conspirators just hours before government troops were dispatched to arrest them. Summoning his parishioners on the 16th, Hidalgo, together with a small band of followers advanced on San Miguel where they were joined by Allende's regiment. The revolutionaries then marched on to the city of Guanajuato, which had a population of 80,000 and some of the richest silver mines in the Americas. It was at the time the second wealthiest city in Mexico. After a desperate siege, the city fell into the hands of the revolutionaries. Hidalgo then turned his forces on Mexico City. Despite routing the Spanish battalion and with the capital in his sights, Hidalgo retreated for some unaccountable reason. Moving towards the interior of the country he encountered 10,000 well equipped government troops at Atulco. Again Hidalgo's leadership proved disastrous and his army was badly mauled.

By this time the government and Church had begun fighting back. The bishop of the state of Michoacan excommunicated the insurgents and the Holy Inquisition (still operating in Mexico) charged Hidalgo and his followers with treason. A reward was offered for his capture, dead or alive.

Hidalgo retreated to Guanajuato, where he published a decree abolishing slavery. He suffered another defeat defending the city, before marching north where he hoped to get supplies and military assistance from the southern states of America. But on March 21st 1811, at Acatita in Chihuahua State, Hidalgo, Allende and Aldama were captured and taken to Chihuahua City where they were executed. Their severed heads were returned to Guanajuato in cages and displayed above the city's walls as a warning to other potential rebels.

A fellow priest and former student of Hidalgo, Jose María Morelos, kept the revolt alive. He proved to be a brilliant leader and tactician. In 1813, he installed the first National Congress and published a decree declaring Mexico an independent republic, but two years later, he too was captured by government troops and hanged. Leadership of his forces passed to one of his lieutenants, Vicente Guerrero, who continued the fight in the rugged mountains of the south. Finally, on February 24th 1821, after years of bitter fighting, General Iturbide, head of the pro-Spanish forces, met Guerrero to discuss the possibility of independence. After protracted negotiations, at Iguala,

Mexico was declared an independent, constitutional monarchy with the throne being offered to a member of a reigning European family. The Iguala agreement upheld the Roman Catholic religion and offered equal citizenship to all the inhabitants of New Spain. Although the viceroy opposed the decision, it proved popular and by the end of 1821, when Iturbide and Guerrero entered the capital, Spanish rule in Mexico had come to an end.

***

In Valle, Independence Day festivities began on the 15th of September, when everyone took to the streets to eat, drink and dance before gathering in the square to hear the mayor address the town with those familiar words first uttered by Hidalgo.

Preparations for the fiesta began a week before. Red, white and green lights – the colours of the Mexican flag were erected in the streets leading into Valle and the town centre. On every street corner stalls appeared selling Mexican flags and clay figurines of Hidalgo. On the night of the 15th, the traditional dish of *pozole* was served (a thick soup containing chunks of *chicharon*, corn, coriander garlic, celery, radishes, onion, lime-juice and dried tortillas). The town's bars and restaurants were packed out, with extra tables and chairs spilling onto the streets where eager *Mariachi* bands waited to attract customers to hire them by the song. Mariachi bands consisted of three to 15 musicians all dressed in full *charro* attire; large sombreros, tight black studded trousers, waistcoats, cowboy boots and spurs. They played guitars of all sizes, trumpets and double basses.

Under the colonnades surrounding the square, old Mazahua women crouched on embroidered mats selling egg shells stuffed with confetti to throw into the crowd at the *Grito*, whilst a band played traditional ranch songs from the bandstand. By 11 o'clock, the crowds gathered in the square and surrounding streets were an inebriated mass of swaying bodies and hands clutching tequila and beer bottles. Fireworks in the inky black sky exploded into red and green showering the town in sparks. And then at five minutes to midnight, the mayor stepped out onto the town hall balcony dressed in his robes of office and a sudden hush fell on the square. He unrolled the traditional scroll upon which Hidalgo's words had been immortalised and as the clock struck midnight, the 16th of September, a simultaneous cry of 'Viva Mexico! Viva la independencia!' burst from the people echoing others all over the republic.

CHAPTER 6

EL DISTRITO FEDERAL

It's Saturday morning and I am playing at Peter Davey's house in *La Herradura*. I like playing at Peter's. His father has a rifle and a revolver and he takes out the bullets and lets us play with them. Peter's mum is out and we are left with the maid. Peter tells me that they are building lots of houses up the road. There are big holes where diggers have been excavating the earth and the holes are full of water. He says they make perfect pools and you can jump off the diggers into the muddy water. The workmen have not been for ages on account of the rains. We close the door quietly behind us and run up the road. The diggers look like yellow dinosaurs. Peter strips off leaving only his white pants on and jumps off a digger into the pool. I follow. The water is cold and muddy and full of grit. We make mud pies and throw them at the still, silent dinosaurs.

***

Mexico City today with its population of 21 million and its choking pollution bears no resemblance to the *Aztec* city of *Tenochtitlan*, described by *Bernal Diaz, Cortés'* chronicler, as 'Even more beautiful than Venice.' **1***

It was in the D.F – *El Distrito Federal* – that I had my first encounter with Mexican bureaucracy. My parents had sent out a rucksack containing camping and mountaineering gear from England and a month after my arrival I had to go to Mexico City to see it through customs. I took the day off work and caught an early bus. I was in the city by 10 o'clock and at the airport an hour later. The journey itself had been uneventful but on arriving at the airport I was surprised to find that no one could give me accurate directions to the customs house.

'Sure, friend,' said a security guard, 'it's opposite the Hertz rental desk over there.' It wasn't.

'Customs?' asked the pretty *Aerolinas Mexicana* official, 'yes it's upstairs on the left next to immigration. Have a nice day.'

Eventually after asking several other people, I found it. A refuse collector, seeing confusion written all over my face as I stood outside the airport terminal offered to walk me in the right direction. It was situated half a mile away behind some aircraft hangers and warehouses.

The scene inside was Kafkaesque. Manned by a harassed staff of two, the dimly lit room was a heaving mass of people. There were papers everywhere: piled up on desks, on the floor, in trays, sticking out of people's pockets, held up in sweaty hands and blowing about by the rusty, dissolute fan that revolved slowly in the ceiling.

There were supposed to be two queues, one to register and another to process customs papers. In reality there was no such order – just a tiny room packed with people shouting and gesticulating. After standing for 15 minutes in the crowded doorway, I asked the woman in front of me whether I had come to the right place.

'Ask that man in the red shirt,' she replied. 'He's been here two days.'

Ramón had come from *Acapulco* to collect a consignment of sports goods from Guatemala. He had been waiting ever since.

'I'll get my footballs sometime,' he said smiling meekly. 'I've no energy left to complain.' He pointed to a small kiosk across the courtyard. 'First you need to get a ticket from there. It has a number on it. Then you come back here and wait your turn.' I had not even noticed the kiosk.

By the time I was back in the queue, there were more than 20 people in front of me with tickets they had obtained the previous day. Number 120 was being processed. The numbers went up to 200 and then returned to zero.

'I wouldn't bother waiting around,' *Ramón* advised. 'The office closes in an hour.'

By now it was two o'clock. I had been there three hours. Frustrated I returned to Valle. I could have saved time and stayed in a hotel but I had had enough of the crowds and the seething traffic. By the time I got to the bus station, my eyes were stinging from the pollution and I had a splitting headache.

The following morning I was at the customs by 10 o'clock. At 12 I finally reached the desk. *Ramón* was still waiting patiently after three days.

'There have been complications with my papers. I did not get this pink facsimile copied,' he said, holding it up.

Having paid 250 pesos in customs fees I was given instructions to pick up my rucksack from warehouse B401. There I had to pay another fee, this time for storage.

'Wait here and someone will get your bag for you,' said the clerk behind the desk. I waited and waited. First 15 minutes, then half an hour and then an hour passed. I was beginning to feel pleased with myself for remaining so relaxed. Just then, a chubby man wearing an oily boilersuit drove up on a forklift truck.

'We cannot find your bag,' he said apologetically. 'Can you help us locate it?'

I exploded. Two days of pent up frustration and anger burst out.

'But that's your bloody job. How will I know where the fucking thing is in this place?' He agreed.

In the end I had to help them. It seemed the only way I would ever retrieve my rucksack. After a further half an hour of searching, we found it. It was stacked four shelves up near the ceiling behind *Ramón's* enormous crate of imported footballs from Guatemala.

***

Lying midway between the west coast and the Gulf of Mexico, in the centre of an area of great fertility, is a valley 25 miles wide and 40 miles long. Rising 7,000 feet above sea level, this valley, formally known as *Anhuac* is flanked to the west by *Mount Ajusco* and to the south east by two other volcanoes: *Popocatépetl* (named after an Aztec warrior) and *Ixtazihuatl* (the princess he loved). With fertile fields, shallow lakes, plentiful water and a temperate climate, the valley now called *El Valle de Mexico* was once the centre of the Aztec empire.

The story of how Hernán Cortés with an army of less than 1000 men, conquered this mighty king-

EL DISTRITO FEDERAL

dom ruled by *Moctezuma,* is one of the greatest adventures of all time.

Between 1492 and 1519, Spanish adventurers had begun exploring the Caribbean and the northern coast of South America. In 1517, an expedition organised by *Diego de Velazquez*, the governor of Cuba, landed on the Yucatán coast and a second expedition a few months later, explored the Gulf coast up to the present day port of *Veracruz.* Both expeditions reported rumours of a fabulous city that lay inland whose streets were paved with gold. Prompted by these reports, Velazquez outfitted an elaborate expedition commanded by Cortés to explore the interior of the country. From the outset, the expedition was plagued by uncertainties. Velazquez distrusted Cortés and planned to have him removed as leader, but Cortés, in a surprise move, set off without permission. His force included 408 infantrymen, 302 archers, 13 musketeers, 16 horses for the officers and 200 Cuban pack bearers. The expedition landed on the island of *Cozumel* near the tip of Yucatán and then sailed north along the Gulf coast. Two events of great importance occurred during this stage of the adventure. At Cozumel, the Spaniards rescued *Jerónimo Aguilar*. Aguilar, a priest, had been captured by *indigenas* during a previous expedition and had lived among them long enough to learn the *Mayan* language. Further up the coast in what is now the state of *Tabasco*, the Spaniards defeated an indigena war party and, as part of their booty, were presented with 20 young girls. Among them was a handsome, intelligent woman called *Malinche*, who eventually became Cortés' mistress. She spoke Maya and Nahuatl, the language of the Aztecs. Combining her talents and Aguilar's knowledge, the Spaniards had expert interpreters and guides.

Cortés reached the island of *San Juan Ulua* on Maundy Thursday, April 21st 1519. A short distance up the coast they founded their first settlement, calling it *La Via Rica de la Vera Cruz*. Here Cortés had his ships burned so that there could be no retreat from the adventure.

Meanwhile, disturbing accounts about the arrival of a race of white men had already reached the Aztec capital. The Aztecs believed that the Spaniards and their horses were demigods and these strangers to their land seemed to confirm an ancient prophecy that *Quetzalcoatl*, the god of their forefathers, would one day return to conquer the country. These beliefs and accompanying fears, combined to aid the Spaniards significantly in their conquest.

After two months of bitter fighting with various jungle tribes, reckless courage and deft diplomacy, the small Spanish force found itself on the 12,000 foot pass between the volcanoes Ixtazihuatl and Popocatepetl. Beneath them lay Tenochtitlan, the Aztec capital – 'A jewel set in the glistening waters of Lake *Texococo*,' Bernal Diaz wrote.

On November the 8th 1519, without having fought a single engagement with Moctezuma's forces, Cortés entered the capital. He was received reluctantly by the Aztec ruler, who came to meet him seated in a jewelled canopy carried on the shoulders of his nobles. Cortés and his officers were lodged in the ancient palace of *Atzayactl*.

Aware that this welcome would not endure and to guarantee the safety of his small force, Cortés persuaded Moctezuma to take up residence among the Spaniards, thus becoming a voluntary hostage.

Shortly after his arrival in Tenochtitlan, news reached Cortés that a force of 1,200 Spaniards sent from Cuba by Governor Velazquez, had arrived in Veracruz to arrest him for mutiny and treason. Leaving a small garrison behind, Cortés hurried to meet this new threat. He encountered Velazquez's army at *Zempoala,* overcame them and persuaded many of the soldiers to join forces with him.

In Tenochtitlan, the Spaniards, under the command of hot-headed *Pedro de Alvarado* had provoked the local citizens. According to a contemporary Aztec account, Alvarado had given the chief Aztec priests permission to prepare a fiesta in honour of one of their gods, during which, human hearts would be sacrificed. While the Aztecs were performing their rituals, Alvarado's men attacked. They sprang into the temple plaza and butchered unarmed worshippers and looted jewellery from the dead and mutilated corpses. Cortés and his men, returning from Zempoala, had to fight their way back into the city where they found the Spanish garrison under siege. Alvarado claimed to have launched a pre-emptive attack, having intercepted a communiqué indicating that the Aztecs planned to attack. The following day when the Aztecs resumed their assault, Cortés persuaded Moctezuma to go onto the roof of the palace and appeal to his people for peace.

The Aztec chieftain was accused of cowardice and was showered with stones and arrows by his own people. He died from his wounds a few hours later. Moctezuma's nephew, a young warrior called *Cuauhtémoc*, then mounted a full scale siege. On June 20th, 1520, a date that has been immortalised in Mexican history as *El Noche Triste*, the Spaniards and heir *Tlaxcalan* allies, retreated from the city.

Loading themselves with gold and jewels given to them in better times by the Aztecs, they set out across the causeways connecting the city to the mainland. The alerted Aztecs attacked in force from small boats. Badly mauled in the nightmare fighting, the Spaniards had to abandon their treasures, their gun-powder and canons. More than 800 Spaniards, 80 horses and thousands of indigena allies were killed during the long night.

The survivors retreated to *Tlaxcala*, where among friends, they were able to rest, re-equip and prepare for another attack upon the Aztec stronghold. At last, strengthened by new arrivals from Cuba, Cortés laid siege to Tenochitlan.

Cuitlahuac, the Aztec leader, had died during an outbreak of smallpox. His successor, Cuauhtémoc, bitterly rejected Cortés' offer of peace. On August 13th 1521, the Spaniards overcame the city, which they razed and levelled. More than three centuries were to pass before the western hemisphere would again see a city of such splendour.*3

CHAPTER 7

EL CINE

The smog gives mum headaches so she has to rest in the afternoon. I sit with *Alberto* in the utility room watching him shine shoes. He is going back to *Oaxaca* next week to visit his family. It takes a whole day to get to his village. *Juventino* will drive him to the bus station. The bus to Oaxaca takes eight hours, and then he has to take another bus. One of his brothers will meet him with two donkeys. They will ride across the sierra to his village.

***

I met *Francisco* the day after my excursion to Mexico. He was the owner of one of Valle's two cinemas and seeing me sitting in a roadside restaurant he had come up and introduced himself.

Francisco did not walk so much as creep in a slow, silent manner, his trousers pulled up around his navel; his shoulders hunched forward, his back bent giving the impression that he had no neck.

'Do you like sexy films?' he asked me in Spanish. 'We are showing 'Basic Instinct' starring Sharon Stone. She is very beautiful and it's a really sexy film.'

Francisco drew up a chair and ordered a strawberry milkshake. He began telling me about his recent trip to London.

'I discovered a really good way to avoid paying for a bus ticket and it worked every time.'

I knew that he was itching to tell me how, but I gave him no encouragement and continued to eat my lunch of meat balls and spaghetti.

'You get on the bus and you sit upstairs on the front seat. The secret is to pretend that you are asleep, but you hold the stub of an old ticket in your fingers. When the conductor comes along he will see the ticket and presume that you have paid.'

A week later, Francisco invited me for lunch. He lived with his twin brother on *La Peña*. La Peña was a rocky peninsular that jutted out of Valle into the lake. It enjoyed one of the finest views in the area. Twenty years ago, there were no houses on the rock. Development was forbidden because La Peña was designated as a sacred historical site. At its base were the ruins of an ancient pyramid, where in pre-Hispanic times, the Aztecs had performed human sacrifices to the god of fertility. It was also an area of outstanding beauty. But five years before I returned to Valle, a millionaire with friends in the government wanted to build his house on the summit of La Peña. No one opposed him and the building of his stately palace, which included a helicopter pad, tennis court, swimming pool and private jetty for his 20 foot motor launch opened the floodgates to other millionaires with friends in high places.

Looking through Francisco's dining room window, past his terraced garden and down to the double garage where two white Mercedes were parked, I wondered why he of all people needed to fare dodge in London.

***

VIVA MEXICO!

There has been a cinema in Valle for over 50 years. When my parents lived in Mexico during the 1970's and we spent our holidays in the town, going to see a film was always a treat. I remember seeing 'Young Winston,' when I was eight years old. There was a group of Mazahua boys sitting in the row in front of us and they cheered exuberantly when young Winston, played by the actor Simon Ward, charged sabre flashing through a legion of whirling Dervishes.

When I returned to Valle there were two cinemas. At weekends, foreign, mostly American films were shown with Spanish subtitles. During the week, the programme was dedicated to the screening of Mexican films, in which the men were all brawny and moustached and carried machine guns and the women were all pout, bust and legs and ready for anything.

Film showings were fraught with disruptions, resulting in a cacophony of catcalls from the mainly male audience. The usual sequence of events during a film was as follows:

- Film begins in the middle
- Film stops and is re-wound

EL CINE

- Part of film melts on screen
- Lights come back on accompanied by catcalls
- There's an impromptu interval
- Film begins again but there is no sound
- Sound comes on but you can only see the actors' legs
- Focus is finally corrected
- Film ends and everyone emerges from the cinema with bits of popcorn in their hair and their legs covered in flea bites.

∽

CHAPTER 8

UNA VISTA

My best friend at school is an American boy called Randy. He is really good at baseball. Jason says that Randy is a naughty word. I said it isn't – it's short for Randolph.

***

A week after I returned to Valle, I set out one afternoon to re-discover the town. Calle de la Culebra was roughly located in the centre of Valle on a hill overlooking the lake. I walked down the cobbled street and turning right up Pagaza, I headed towards the square. Here there were boutiques selling jewellery and clothes, pottery and handmade arts and crafts. On reaching the square I passed a bike shop and peered in. Two mechanics were busy servicing bikes; oiling chains, re-setting gears and tightening bolts and racked up against the wall were familiar brands: Specialised, Giant, Ridgeback and others. The square was much as I remembered it. There were restaurants, a bakery, a couple of ironmongers, the bookshop and a chemist and towering over it was the majestic church of *San Francisco*. I headed north along Calle Revolución where old women shelled nuts and knitted in their open doorways. Here there were garages and an eclectic mix of shops selling agricultural implements, animal feed, wall tiles and *serapes*. The road continued up through *Ottumba* and Tierras Blancas to the school, but I turned left and walked towards the post office and *Banamex*, one of Valle's three banks. It looked meticulous and incongruously clean, behind plate glass doors. Inside, the air was scented with air freshener, clerks all wore pristine blue suits and the marble floor glistened like polished glass.

I made my way towards the market and spotted Tonio at his stove and then headed down to the lake. Mazahua women sat cross legged on the pavements with their ponchos and brightly coloured waistcoats and a man selling candy floss walked lethargically up and down the pier. An itinerant salesman sold pine furniture from the back of a truck and fishermen threw freshly caught trout from their boats into buckets of ice on the dock. I followed the lakeside road and found myself in the old barrio of Santa Maria with its church of honey coloured stone and quiet streets. Here there were weekend houses owned by millionaires and politicians behind high walls and gates with intercoms. I passed the prestigious Santa Maria Sailing Club where a disgraced former president had once been a member. Pristine yachts and motor launches bobbed up and down on the water. Small boys in straw hats sold ocote and wood on the sidewalk and teenagers on quad bikes and motorcycles raced by. Above Valle, five paragliders hovered like primeval birds over the town. I stopped and watched as one gracefully spiralled down and landed on marshy ground near the water. I walked past the *Lagartija club,* less luxurious than the Santa Maria Club, but nonetheless a popular playground for the capital's rich elite. Out on the lake there were sailboats and jet skis. I headed back towards the Culebra, passing the Blackmore's house and heard Nancy in animated conversation with her neighbour. I wanted to get a view of the whole of Valle so I climbed up through a myriad of medieval alleyways that followed a brook to the top of the hill behind the town. Here there were corrugated shanties and chickens pecking in the mud. I passed the last house and took a dirt track that wove its way between pine trees a further two miles to a fire tower. The climb was steep and muddy and I stopped twice to catch my breath and admire the view below before reaching the treeless summit. I sat on a stump and watched the paraglider pilots launch themselves off the hill, their chutes billowing open as they drifted out and over the lake. Below, lay Valle. I spotted the pink arch at the entrance to the town. I could see the bandstand in the square, the market and the two churches. I followed Pagaza to the foot of Culebra to try to spot my house but it was obscured by Josefina's large terrace.

The view in the early evening sun was spectacular. Beyond were the hills of Guerrero and Michoacan. The sun was sinking slowly behind the hamlet of *Cerrillo* at the western end of the lake and it cast a prism of golden light over the water. To the south rose the wooded peaks and valleys of Cerro Gordo from where plumes of blue wood smoke rose from distant ranches.

As I began my descent, the skies suddenly darkened and thunder rumbled through the sierra.

And then the heavens opened and it poured sweet smelling rain and I was drenched to the skin.

༼ ༽

CHAPTER 9

LA TERTULIA

We received a letter from Lucinda yesterday from boarding school. She's homesick and misses *Adela, Alberto* and *Pancho*. Her best friend is a girl called Louise. Her parents used to have a pet lion. They are actors and were in the film 'Born Free.' Lucinda says she will bring us some packets of Smarties when she comes back at Christmas. She is in the netball team.

***

I had been in Valle six weeks when I decided to hold a party to get to know my work colleagues in a more relaxed setting. I had been employed to co-ordinate the small English department which consisted of me, Mark and two Mexican women: Milli Grimaldi and *Elisa Alcocer*.

Milli was married to Sal, an Italian Canadian. She had been born and brought up in Mexico but had left for a new life in Canada in her early twenties and she had only just returned to Valle. She and her husband lived above the school in a house that they had built with their own hands with a garden centre attached, which Sal ran in his retirement.

Sal had wiry grey hair, clear blue eyes and weathered skin. He had been an engineer spending much of his career drilling for oil in the Arctic and in the deserts of Northern Mexico and Arizona. He dabbled at being an artist in his free time and their house was littered with half finished canvases depicting polar scenes and barren landscapes.

'I watched a man die in *Chihuahua* State from a scorpion sting,' he said by way of an introduction. 'We were camped by a river and I had just lit a fire and put coffee on after our evening meal, when I heard someone screaming near the river. This great big bull of a man, one of the guys on our team, his name escapes me now, came running up clutching his huge, swollen hand. He'd been stung on the finger by a 'guerro' – one of the small, almost transparent scorpions, that inhabit Northern Mexico, but it packs enough poison to kill a horse.

We were miles from a hospital and had no means of getting to one. Within 24 hours the poor man was dead. We buried him in the desert. It took three men 10 hours to dig his grave in the hard, rocky soil. I remember the day. It was the 29th June 1958!'

Milli was in her early fifties. She wore her long blonde hair piled up in a bun and looked more Scandinavian than Mexican. She was passionate about music and in addition to teaching English, she taught the children the recorder and guitar and was in charge of the small but burgeoning school choir. She spoke perfect English with a slight French Canadian accent. I quickly discovered that Milli had a wonderful sense of humour and when she and Sal had had a drink they were great company.

Elisa Alcocer didn't look Mexican either. She looked quintessentially English with a pale complexion, high cheek bones and dark blonde hair. She was in her early forties and was married to a politician who was permanently on the campaign trail and whom she rarely saw. She had two sons in the school, *Constanino* and *Emiliano*. Like Milli, Elisa was also bilingual but spoke English with a charming Mexican accent. Elisa had been one of the first teachers to be recruited after the school's humble beginnings.

The remainder of the staff were all Mexican, mostly from Valle. There was *Ilda* who headed the Spanish department and her brother *Mario*, a surly looking young man who resented me from the moment I set foot in the school and never spoke to Mark. *Rocio*, also a Spanish teacher was married to *Carlos* a local vet. *Sirani*, a *Tarahumara* from Chihuahua reminded me of an exotic tropical bird. She worked in the kindergarten and took every opportunity to practise her English with Mark and me. She came from a remote village in the Copper Canyon and was proud of her people, particularly their legendary stamina and running ability.

'Tarahumara boys learn to run great distances barefoot through the dry canyon from an early age. When a boy reaches puberty, he has to enter a running race with the men of the tribe. They run through the dry river beds kicking wooden footballs in a relay race that covers 160 miles of barren terrain. My people were never subdued by the Spaniards. When the white men came from Europe, the Tarahumara left their homes on the plains and took refuge in the canyon living in caves and in small remote communities,' she told us.

Rosa ran the pre-school nursery. She was small with auburn hair and a beaky nose. She had an infectious laugh and told the most disgusting jokes and stories and was the life and soul of any party. She lived just up the road from me at the end of *Culebra*. In addition to teaching, Rosa edited the local newspaper, had her own show on the Valle radio and spent her free time sitting in the square reading to the local children. She had boundless energy and a ribald sense of humour.

Maria also worked in the pre-school nursery and was married to *Andres* Austin, a car mechanic. They had three children in the school and lived in a dusty village called *Rincon de Estradas* half an hour's drive out of Valle in cactus country. The house was infested with scorpions and was falling down and the roof leaked in the rainy season but the children loved it. And then there was Alejandra Gerrard who captained this motley crew. She was five feet, two inches tall with dark shoulder length hair and round spectacles. Alejandra was married to *Fabian* who was rumoured to be an arms dealer. Shortly after I arrived in Valle, Alejandra invited me for lunch to talk about the English department. As I sat in the living room sipping a cold *Corona* beer, I flicked through the selection of coffee table magazines which included copies of 'Jane's Defence Weekly' and 'Soldier of Fortune,' a specialist publication for mercenaries, advertising martial arts equipment, survival courses, guns and companies offering close personal protection.

There was certainly no shortage of money in the family. The Gerrards owned a mansion in Valle with its own private jetty, a huge ranch on the southern end of the lake and property in Mexico City.

I had prepared food for half past seven but no one arrived before eight o'clock. Mark was the first to knock on my gate. He handed me a bottle of Bacardi and a six pack of beer. He apologised for being on 'Mexican time' and warned me that Mexican colleagues would probably not show up until 10 o'clock. We sat in front of the fire and drank a few beers savouring the combination of cold lager and freshly squeezed lime juice. Mark told me about Isabel Brown, a co-founder of the school (and a neighbour of mine) who had had two sons in the school the previous year. She had since moved back to Mexico City and her sons were now in the British school.

'Her eldest son, Travis is an extremely talented guitarist and has already performed in concerts all over Mexico but he's your typical spoilt rich Mexican teenager. When he was at the school last year, I regularly caught him smoking behind the science lab. Once he knew that I was on to him, I think he had it in for me. After school one afternoon, I discovered a pile of horse shit in my car. I knew Travis had done it; and he knew that I knew he had done it but I was powerless. Isabel flatly refused to believe me. When I threatened to hand in my notice and leave mid way through the term, other members of staff, (notably Ilda) came out and supported me and told Isabel that her precious little son was actually a toe rag. I think Isabel took the kids out of school to pre-empt Travis being expelled!'

Mark downed his Corona; the smile had gone from his face.

'A word of advice, Marcus – you can take it or leave it; don't get on the wrong side of rich, wealthy Mexicans, even if you know you are in the right. They wield enormous power in this country and can make your life hell if you cross them. They are like the mafia!'

An hour later, the other guests arrived. Soon the house was full. I knew about half the people; the rest were friends of friends or relatives of staff who had come along for the party. No one touched the food but everyone drank. There were empty Bacardi, beer and Tequila bottles everywhere and the distinct, pungent smell of marijuana. Milli had brought her guitar and started playing Edith Piaff songs. Sal got quietly drunk and began dancing the Polka alone in a corner, a thick cigar clutched between his fingers whilst Rosa held court and told obscene jokes. Carlos pushed back the sofa and chairs and someone put on a *Salsa* tape and the dancing began.

Andres got steadily more and more inebriated as the evening wore on and a man, whom I had never met before, kept telling me what a wonderful party it was and that I was '*muy buena onda.*' He too was drunk and spent most of the time slapping people on the back or kissing women and telling everyone how much he loved them.

Andres asked me if I wanted to buy a second hand car.

'It's a good'un and real low on mileage. I'll bring it around tomorrow if you like.' We set a time and he drifted onto the subject of smoking weed.

'When Michael is 13, I will give him his first joint,' he said proudly.' 'All this about it leading on to harder drugs is just so much horse shit,' he insisted. Michael was his 11 year old son.

At about three o'clock in the morning people began drifting home. Hardly any of the food I had prepared had been eaten and the house stank of alcohol and smoke and there was ash down the side of the sofa and all over my rugs. But the party, everyone said, had been a success.

'Do it again,' Elisa said on leaving. 'This kind of thing is good for staff morale and prevents people from gossiping.'

***

VIVA MEXICO!

The following day, Sunday, I waited in for Andres. We had arranged to meet at my house at midday. Andres' parents were British but he had spent all his life in Mexico. Maria, his wife was second generation Mexican. Her grandparents had been Italian immigrants. Andres was deeply tanned with a short beard and long chin. Apart from his blonde hair there was nothing to indicate his British lineage. He spoke English with a Mexican American accent and had only been to the United Kingdom once. In fact he despised everything that was British.

'The weather was shit, the food was shit and the women looked like shit!' he explained. 'Why would I ever want to go back?'

***

At one 0'clock the following day, Andres still had not arrived. I waited another hour and then decided to lock up and go for a walk.

I strolled down Pagaza and flagged a taxi going to Avandaro. I asked to be taken to *La Vela de la Novia*, a popular picnic spot by the side of a dramatic waterfall. From there a dirt track led 3 miles to the village of *Cerro Gordo*. These were places I had visited as a child. Memories of riding through these woods came flooding back as I retraced my steps. The path wound gently through pine forest, passing small hamlets of corrugated iron shacks. Several horsemen rode past leading mules laden with timber and grain. At a junction there was a sign carved into a tree and directions for *El Pinal,* another mountain settlement. I took the southern fork to Cerro Gordo. The track grew progressively muddier. At one point a car had got stuck. There was mud and water up to the doors. The driver and six other men were trying to pull it out using two mules. They slipped and cursed but eventually they dragged the filthy car out of the mire. The engine was clogged up and wouldn't start.

Cerro Gordo consisted of a collection of small farms, a white washed chapel and a general store. Children, pigs and chickens ran about and women laid out laundry to dry on cacti. I sat down in a field of wild flowers to admire the view of Valle below, nestled in on the side of the lake. There were white sails on the water and a single paraglider hovered high above the town like a bird. I recalled how years before my sister

Fiona and Maria Freitag had got lost riding in these woods. They were gone for hours. A posse of ranch hands and muleteers had accompanied my father in searching for the two girls and then, just as it was beginning to get dark, they appeared through the trees singing 'Puff the Magic Dragon' oblivious of the panic and worry their absence had caused.

***

On Monday after school I met Andres at the school gate. He had come to collect his children.

'What happened about our meeting yesterday? Weren't you going to bring the car around?' I asked him.

'Oh yeah! I kinda forgot. *Manolo* came around and we drank some beers and smoked some joints; but hey, how about some time this week?'

CHAPTER 10

LA MATANZA DE TLATELOLCO

We learned today in school that in the old days here in Mexico people were sacrificed to the gods. Their hearts were cut out so that there woud be a good harvest. Mum said I shouldn't be afraid because it doesn't happen now.

***

In early October, liberal Mexicans commemorated the 25th anniversary of the *Tlatelolco* massacre that took place in Mexico City in 1968, days before the opening of the Olympic Games.

In the summer of 1968, Mexico was experiencing the birth of a new student movement. It was short lived. On October 2nd, a week before the Olympics were due to start, police officers and troops shot into a crowd of unarmed students. Thousands of demonstrators fled in panic as tanks bulldozed over Tlatelolco Plaza.

Government sources originally reported that four people had been killed and 20 wounded, while eyewitnesses described the bodies of hundreds of young people being trucked away. Thousands of students were beaten and jailed, and many vanished altogether. Twenty five years later, the final death toll remained a mystery, but documents recently released by the U.S. and Mexican governments give a better picture of what may have triggered the massacre. These documents suggest that snipers posted by the military fired on fellow troops, provoking them to open fire on the students.

In 1968, student movements were sprouting up all over the world — including France, Germany, Italy, Czechoslovakia, Argentina, Japan and the United States. Mexico, like many countries in the prosperous 1960s, had spawned a vibrant middle class that enjoyed a quality of life unimaginable in previous decades. These children of the Mexican Revolution that now lived in comfort were, for the first time, able to send their own children to university in unprecedented numbers.

The student movement had its first confrontation with the authorities during a riot after a football game. The police were sent in to end the skirmish and after hours of resistance, the army arrived to quell the violence. The siege ended when the soldiers blasted the main door of the National Preparatory School in *San Ildefonso* with a bazooka, killing a number of the students in the building.

The National University oversaw the Preparatory School, so the involvement of university officials was inevitable. In the following hours, the students decided to protest against the violence exerted by the riot police. Over the following months, Mexico City witnessed a series of demonstrations and rallies.

Everyone expected the government to give in to their demands, but they were greeted with a clear message from the president: 'No more unrest will be tolerated,' the newspapers reported. The army proceeded in the following days to seize the National University, with virtually no resistance, and later the National Polytechnic, where they were met with violent student protest.

Following these tumultuous events, the students rapidly called for a new gathering on October 2nd at the Three Cultures Square in the Tlatelolco housing complex. Thousands gathered to hear first hand from the movement's leaders what resistance they planned next. As the gathering was ending, soldiers arrived to arrest the movement's leaders. They were greeted by gunshots from the buildings surrounding the square. The troops then opened fire, turning the evening into a massacre that lasted nearly two hours.

Over the following days, the official account of the events would be that the students — infiltrated by communist forces — had fired on the army, and soldiers had returned fire in self defence. Under the authoritarian regime of President *Gustavo Diaz Ordaz*, no formal investigation into the killings was ever conducted. The number of civilian casualties reported ranged between four — in the official count directly after the event — and 3,000. Eyewitnesses recounted seeing dozens of bodies and prisoners being trucked away to military bases. But despite efforts by both the student leaders and the special prosecutor to compile the names of the dead, only about 40 have ever been documented. No siblings, parents or friends of the remaining casualties — if they still existed — ever came forward to add names to the list.

Many believe that the Presidential Guard — a branch of the military — had posted snipers on the buildings surrounding Tlatelolco Plaza on the day of the protest and that these same snipers provoked the ensuing chaos by deliberately firing on troops. The soldiers, thinking they had been attacked by the students opened fire indiscriminately on the crowd.

The terrible events of that day were still an open sore in the psyche of many middle aged Mexicans who in their youth had witnessed a burgeoning student movement so brutally crushed and they still sought the truth to unanswered questions. Who was responsible for ordering the shootings? What had happened to a generation of young men and women who simply disappeared that day never to be seen or heard of again? And how many of their student comrades had actually been killed?

Many still suspected that the Americans (and the CIA in particular) were indirectly responsible for the massacre. Fearful of a growing Marxist movement on its doorstep and paranoid about security arrangement for such a high profile international event, it was believed that the U.S had provided not only logistical support in suppressing the movement but also arms and vital intelligence. Twenty five years on Mexicans were still seeking answers to the question of what really happened on *La noche de Tlatelolco*.

༄

CHAPTER 11

LAS LLUVIAS

Juventino used to play professional football before he started working for the bank. Now he drives dad to work. I've watched him do 100 kick-ups in his smart black shoes, wearing a suit. He was a long distance lorry driver too. Mum says he shouldn't eat from street stalls because he is often ill. Last year he had hepatitis.

***

Tlaloc was the Aztec god of rain. In a country where the success of the crops rested on the annual rainfall, he was a deity of high importance. The Aztecs believed quite logically, that Tlaloc made his home in the Valley of Mexico since, the surrounding hills and veil of mist that obscured their summits were the source of the local rainfall. His popularity was also vouched for by the fact that there were more sculptured representations of him than any other god.

It is said that the rainy season in Mexico lasts five months and that it begins and ends on the same day every year: the fifth of May and the fourth of October. So, when I arrived in Valle in late August, it was the middle of the rainy season.

Every afternoon at about two o'clock, the skies would darken and a flash of lightning above the mountains followed by the distant rumbling of thunder would herald the arrival of the day's rain.

When it rained there was only one way to remain dry: run for the cover of four solid walls and a roof. Umbrellas and fancy waterproofs were useless. Umbrellas, however robust, would crumple under the weight and volume of water and waterproofs would begin to resemble wet tissue paper in minutes. When it rained there was water everywhere. It gushed off rooftops and filled gutters overflowing into shops and houses. It sought out holes in my roof with a maddening drip. When it rained the streets were transformed into streams of muddy water and thunder and lightning would echo about the mountains for hours.

During a meeting at the school one afternoon, a bolt of lightning struck the driveway with a bomb-like blast. Sparks and lumps of tarmac flew into the air like shrapnel. The pre-Hispanic gods of rain and thunder demand respect.

In 1975, we were out riding in the meadows above Cerro Gordo when we were caught in a torrential downpour. Phillip Mayberry, a close friend of my parents was crossing a swollen beck when his horse slipped, throwing Phillip into the swirling waters. His coat snagged on a low hanging branch of a tree and he was able to pull himself free. His horse was washed downstream and drowned, despite desperate efforts to reach it.

A taxi driver taking me home from school one afternoon in the pouring rain described watching a pine tree full of resin being struck by lightning,

'I was looking through the window down my field to the woods beyond when a tree in the garden was hit by lightning. The sound was deafening and I watched as the tree exploded into a ball of fire. Nothing was left of it except the roots. I made the sign of the cross and hoped a bolt of lightning would never hit my house!'

One afternoon in mid September, the Blackmores invited me for lunch. Robert had lent me a key so that I could let myself in through the back garden. By the time I left my house, it was raining heavily. Just as I arrived at the Blackmores' wooden gate I heard a loud gushing, crunching sound and looked up to see a torrent bursting through a pipe and cascading down the hillside bringing mud and all manner of debris with it. The waters were up to my waist in seconds and I could feel my feet being floated off the ground. The gate gave way beneath the weight of water and began flooding into the Blackmore's garden and towards their house taking me with it. I would have drowned and their house washed away, had not their empty swimming pool swallowed up and diverted most of the swell.

***

The fourth of October, *El Dia San de Francisco*, was perhaps the most colourful of Valle's festivals. Not only did it mark the traditional end of the rains; the season of floods and mud that destroyed countless adobe huts, bringing poverty and misery in their wake, but it also honoured the town's patron saint and celebrated animal life.

LAS LLUVIAS

From six in the morning until late in the evening, a steady stream of animal traffic with their *campesino* owners paraded through the streets to the parish church. For a whole day there was the deafening sound of braying donkeys and barking dogs and the thunder of hooves on cobbled streets. The scene was a kaleidoscope of colour: polished leather and yokes adorned with flowers, shiny mule harnesses and bits, ornate saddles and ox drawn carts. Mazahua women wore pink, blue and purple petticoats whilst their men folk sported white smocks and open leather *huaraches* and straw hats. The smell of dung and animals was almost overpowering.

From villages and ranches far away in the hills *campesinos*, *peones* and farmers came to Valle for the one church service in the year when all blessings were for the welfare of their animals. There would be prayers for good breeding and for fatter pigs; prayers for an abundance of milk and eggs and prayers for the health of a valued donkey, sheepdog or chicken. Inside the church, the usually cold stone flags were a carpet of straw and flowers.

It was, for *Padre Ruffo* and the other priests, their busiest day; the only day perhaps when every campesino had a vested interest in attending mass. The blessings could make the difference between a successful and a disastrous year. For Ruffo, a devout Christian, it was a unique opportunity to preach to a full congregation. He would bless the animals and pray for a favourable agricultural year. And then he would preach against avarice, adultery and drunkenness. He would speak about salvation and the duty of all Catholics to attend mass and confession regularly.

In the evening there was a fiesta in the square, where a pole had been erected with the prize of a full sack of maize perched precariously at the top. The beam had been covered in pig fat and the challenge was to scale it and bring down the sack of maize. I watched a young man try to climb it with a pair of rope tourniquet's but two metres off the ground, he lost his grip and came tumbling down to the boos and shrieks of the crowd. Another man tried climbing it using weight lifting gloves but he too got no further than a third of the way up. The prize was eventually won by a team of young men who formed a pyramid. A gangly youth climbed on his teammates' shoulders and lunged for the sack which came toppling down, bringing all six men down with it. They lay in a greasy heap at the bottom laughing hysterically.

At midnight, a *ranchero* band struck up. The singers wore cowboy boots and white shirts, with boot-lace ties tucked into tight black jeans. They sang songs about life on the range, drinking and the women who had broken their hearts.

The clearing up began at three in the morning. The square and streets were awash with animal faeces, wreaths of flowers, empty beer and tequila bottles and the remains of half eaten tacos. But by seven o'clock in the morning on the 5th of October, Valle was spotless again and the stray dogs were settling down to sleep after the best night of pickings in the whole year.

∽

CHAPTER 12

EL ALMUERZO

We went to the George's yesterday for lunch. *Paula* pinched my cheeks so hard I thought I would cry. She kept calling me *'chulito!'* David and Jason climbed onto the roof and set fire to paper planes and threw them into the garden. Kes and I played cowboys and indians. We are going down to *Valle* with them next week. Clare said that *Jesus* will probably take us riding.

***

Once a week, Nancy Blackmore would invite me to lunch. She was keen to hear about my first impressions of the school and to give me some advice.

'You've got an important job here Marcus,' she said, handing me a beer. We were sitting out on the covered terrace watching the black rain clouds roll in over Cerro Gordo.

'Some of the parents need educating as much as their children and the wealthy ones are the worst.'

The Blackmores had been involved in the school from its humble beginnings and Alejandra Gerrard had become a close friend. Both Nancy and Robert were school governors and Nancy was a regular fundraiser, donating the proceeds from her art exhibitions and hosting charity dinners and events among Valle's expatriate community in aid of the school.

Presently, Robert joined us. With his white beard and kind, blue eyes, he reminded me of George Bernard Shaw.

'Nancy's right you know. Some of these wealthy Mexicans have no manners and can be very uncouth. If you can educate their children, you educate the family. The locals are different. They are usually hardworking and grateful for the opportunity of an excellent education.'

Nancy asked after my parents and siblings. The previous year they had toured Spain with my mother and father.

'It was a real hoot!' Nancy exclaimed, 'and your father was such a good guide and a fount of knowledge on everything.'

Robert nodded in agreement. 'We got into a nice little routine. We would usually see a cathedral or an *Alcazar* in the morning and then stop somewhere picturesque for lunch and have a glass of Spanish wine and a *bocadillo* of *Serrano* ham or something. And in the evenings we played Boggle. Your mother is very competitive!'

The Blackmores were amongst my parents' closest friends. Although slightly older and both now in their late 70's, they had befriended my parents when they first arrived in Mexico in 1968 and introduced them to many of their friends and business contacts. In 17 years they had hardly changed. Nancy had a lovely speaking voice; the kind you hear on old black and white films like 'Brief Encounter.' She spoke Spanish fluently but with the same crisp English accent, which often left her Mexican listeners quite baffled and none the wiser! Robert had a deep gravelly voice. He was the quintessential gentleman. Nancy left us for a moment and disappeared into the kitchen.

'We certainly had some good times back in the 70's,' Robert said, nostalgically as he packed his pipe with pungent tobacco. 'The Daly's (referring to us), Georges, Braggs, Wiggs and others. Do you remember the paper chases?' He continued. 'Of course we couldn't do something like that now; leaving trails of confetti all over the pristine forest and allowing our children to ride off into the woods alone or accompanied by a campesino,' he chuckled.

We moved inside for lunch. We began with an avocado and a delicate coriander and soy dressing. Then Nancy rang a little hand bell, and *Esperanza*, the maid appeared bearing a huge Shepherd's pie and a pewter dish with carrots and cabbage.

I had recently returned from a mountain biking expedition to Pakistan's Karakoram Range, and Robert was interested in hearing all about it. I described how David George and I had been stoned out of a village in Chilas and chased by a pack of dogs in the desert.

I asked after their children, who were all older than us. I had clear memories of going to their eldest daughter's wedding in 1974. Rosemary was married to *Carlos*, an engineer by profession.

Robert went on to tell me the harrowing account of how Carlos had disappeared 18 months before.

'He had a big contract to deliver some turbines to a factory up in *Zacatecas* owned by a local politician and then one afternoon as he was leaving the office, a black Suburban with tinted windows stopped and three burly men dressed in dark suits and sun glasses grabbed Carlos and bundled him into the car and sped off. He was gone for days. No one knew where he was or who had kidnapped him.'

Robert re-lit his pipe and paused. Nancy brought in a tray of coffee and a bar of plain chocolate and we moved outside to the covered terrace.

'People like Carlos don't just disappear in Mexico. He's a very successful business man with contacts in high places. Someone somewhere always knows something but all our investigations and enquiries drew a blank. And then one day he turned up dishevelled and in shock. There was no direct proof linking the disappearance to his lucrative Zacatecan contractors but someone had clearly 'lent' on him.'

The rains had ceased and the air smelt clean and crisp. I looked out over the quiet village, the terracotta roofs were glistening wet and I was reminded that Mexico could be a very dangerous place.

***

The end of October brought murder and mayhem to Valle. It began when the headwaiter of one of the town's most popular restaurants was gunned down on the road to Toluca. He had been shopping to buy weekly supplies for the restaurant and was carrying a large quantity of cash. It was never known whether his assailants had been tipped off or whether the attack had been arbitrary, but the violent manner in which the man had been executed suggested that he had been killed by members of a local drug cartel that operated from a remote mountain hamlet called *Coral de Piedra* deep in the *Sierra Madre*.

The murder was the first of nine killings, one rape and several armed robberies that occurred in the vicinity of Valle in the space of a week. All carried the hallmarks of the same group. Sophisticated transportation, weaponery and communication systems had all been used in the assaults and each was designed to intimidate and instil fear.

Two days later, a similar incident took place on the highway in which a motorist died and 10 drivers were robbed. Bandits set up a roadblock along a particularly lonely stretch of the *Amanalco* road. They chose their moment well, just as a convoy of cars was approaching a narrow bend on a mountainous road. The roadblock caused the first vehicle to brake suddenly resulting in a pile up. Whilst cars were prevented from proceeding further down the road, a large truck sandwiched the convoy in from behind preventing escape from the rear. Motorists were then robbed at gunpoint (one was shot when he resisted) before the roadblock was lifted and the highwaymen escaped into the surrounding woods.

Early in October, I had set out from Valle to explore Corral de Piedra. At the time I was unaware that it was a dangerous place; I knew only that it was remote and set in a very beautiful valley at the confluence of the *Temascaltepec* and *Pipioltepec* rivers. To reach it I cycled 20 miles out of Valle on the Toluca road, climbing and twisting through thick woods. After two hours of steep cycling I reached a high plateau. Here, there was an unexpected opening in the forest where a rocky track led elusively across country. Several times I had to ask shepherds for directions, for the plateau was a labyrinth of paths, but I was well received by everyone I met. The path eventually dropped from the high plain through more forest and then crossed a wide river over a log bridge. Here, the woods opened up again at a large ranch with white washed walls and wooden gates. Horses grazed on the upland pastures and a carpet of blue and yellow flowers stretched across the meadows. Around the ranch were some wooden cabins, a small shop and a chapel on which a sign read *'La hermita de Coral de Piedra.'* I had arrived at my destination. I bought a coke and a chocolate bar from the shop and sat outside to admire the view. Getting back on my bike I asked for directions again this time for the town of *Amanalco* on the other side of the valley. A young shepherd pointed to a muddy path that rose up through the forest. I left the ranch and climbed through trees and brush leaving the Pipioltepec River flowing beneath me. A few miles of difficult cycling brought me to the Amanalco Valle road where I waded through the river and began my fast descent home.

Corral de Piedra was probably the ideal place to plan and execute highway robberies. Two major roads bringing weekend traffic to Valle and back to Mexico City flanked the remote valley. It was also difficult to reach, requiring four wheel drive trucks or motorbikes. The bandits had used the natural surroundings to their advantage. They knew that at strategic points along both roads, communication by mobile phone or radio was inhibited by dense woods and high mountains. A police patrol discovered this to its cost after stumbling upon a robbery on the Valle road. A chase ensued, and the police found themselves in unfamiliar country and lost radio contact with their headquarters. When they stopped to study a map of the area, brigands surrounded the car and opened fire on them. One policeman died, another was paralysed from the neck down.

***

On October 26th local residents took to the streets and marched to the town hall to demand protection from the mayor's office. There was a tense atmosphere in the air that was almost tangible. People were frightened, angry and concerned about the crisis on Valle's roads and wanted reassurances from the authorities that measures would be taken to protect them on journeys in and out of the town.

Some believed that corrupt policeman were behind or profiting from the spate of robberies and killings. 'How else do these murderers get hold of such weapons and support if not from the police or army?' shouted one angry protester.

Later that night in a public address on the local radio, the mayor vowed to track down the killers within a month:

'We will apprehend these villains,' he promised.

'That won't happen,' said Rosa, who was reporting on the various incidents for the Valle newspaper, 'not until some rich kid is killed. The government doesn't care about a few *Vallesanos*. It's probably protecting the killers anyway.

All politicians in Mexico have links to the drug cartels. The army will only act if ordered to do so by the government and government is in the pay of the drug barons, and so on and so forth,' she said cynically.

Six weeks later, the police rounded up 20 campesinos living in *Corral de Piedra*, among them women and children and the murders ceased, but no one was happy.

'Those people were not responsible,' said *Laura Lopez*, a local historian. 'All that the local government did was put pressure on the real villains; told them it was bad for business and affecting the tourist industry. The police made a few arrests to give the impression that they are in control, but you watch, as the crisis deepens in this country, there will be more killings.'

CHAPTER 13

EL VAGABUNDO

Inspired by the electrician whom I watch intently, pliers in hand, coiling copper wire in the open garage, I take a single hair clip which I have picked up from somewhere inside the house and push it into the wall socket. I am sitting on a blue tricycle. The red shock passes through the clip, up my hand and arm and I watch it shiver and feel the heat passing through my body and then I am lying on the cold floor, fingers burning, crying.

***

I was born travelling: not in the literal sense but my parents were always on the move. My father worked for The Bank of London and South America and by the time I was born in Buenos Aires, Argentina he had lived or travelled in every country south of the U.S border. He had also travelled and worked extensively in Eastern Europe and Russia.

My father had a fascinating life and my wanderlust and craving for adventure came directly from him. Aged 13, he was offered a scholarship to The King's School, Canterbury and the education he received there mapped out the terrain of his future. Evacuated to Cornwall during the early part of the Second World War, his school days were one long caper; a veritable story from 'The Boys' Own Annual.' Most teachers who were under the age of 45 and reasonably fit were conscripted to fight in Europe or the deserts of North Africa leaving a threadbare staff of doddery 'has beens' or damaged veterans from the Great War in charge of the school in its new surroundings; The Carlyon Bay Hotel, St Austell.

I don't recall my father ever talking about the education he received at school but there were stories of raiding the hotel's larder at night, swimming in the sea in all weathers and accounts of Canon Shirley, the school's charismatic, eccentric headmaster. At the end of one summer term, my father cycled 250 miles home to Woking in

Hampshire, staying in farms along the way and earning his keep hay baling and picking fruit.

When he was 17 and head-boy of the school, he was awarded a scholarship to read History at Trinity College Oxford, but shortly after taking up his place, he joined the Royal Navy. He once described his two years as a sailor in the final years of the war, as 'The true comprehensive university of life,' where men of all classes (and ages) were thrown together briefly and intimately in a common cause.

After the war, he returned to Oxford where he spent much of his time directing and producing plays and opera. He also gained a half blue in boxing (which he had taken up in the navy) and a blue in athletics, on one occasion coming second to Roger Bannister in an inter college meet.

His love of music led him to his first job as an assistant director at Glyndebourne which had recently re-opened after the war (where he worked under Sir Thomas Beecham) but the work was badly paid and he wanted to see more of the world and travel. An Oxford contact put him in touch with a director of the Bank of London and South

America, suggesting that a career in international banking might provide opportunities for extensive travel in the Americas.

Before he met my mother, my father accompanied the chairman of the bank on a number of trips to South America. He took up riding, playing polo in Brazil, Argentina and Uruguay on tough *Pampa* ponies with gauchos and farm workers. Along with music, horses and riding became lifelong passions, the latter of which he enjoyed right up until he died at the age of 78. After he retired he routinely got up at five in the morning and rode with the Horse Guards in Hyde Park. His work with the bank also took him to Russia where he gathered intelligence for MI6. On returning from one trip he was de-briefed by George Blake, who was later exposed as a KGB agent.

My parents met through the bank. My mother was a director's secretary and after just three years of marriage, with two young children in tow, they moved to Argentina for the first of two postings in Buenos Aires. It was an exciting time to be in South America. They were in Buenos Aires when Simon Wiesenthal's Nazi hunters caught up with Adolf Eichmann. Revolution was in the air and *Che Guevara* was captured and executed by CIA assisted agents in Bolivia in 1967, the year after I was born.

In Ecuador my father climbed *Cotopaxi* and other Andean peaks with local mountaineers and both he and my mother embarked on various expeditions into the interior of the country, once staying in a remote jungle lodge owned by a middle aged German with a war scar. They often wondered if he too was an escaped Nazi.

One evening in *Quito* my parents were invited to a reception at the presidential palace. Among the guests were the American ambassador and his wife. She had a penchant for reptiles and turned up to the cocktail party with a boa constrictor around her neck. Half way through the dinner, the president, *Arosemena Monroy*, got drunk, ordered a waiter to place a glass jug on his head, whipped out a nickel plated revolver from his ceremonial holster and shot the jug clean off the man's crown, showering the assembled guests in shards of glass. The following week, he attempted the same trick again and killed a footman. Two months later, he was removed from office by a coupe d'état, led by a military junta.

Years later, in 1979, when my father had been posted to Madrid, he took a covert trip back to Central America, this time volunteering as a hostage negotiator. Two employees of the bank had been kidnapped by a Marxist group known as *Farabundo Marti Nacional* in *El Salvador* and were demanding a huge ransom in exchange for their release. My father knew the country well and the two bank employees were acquaintances. At the age of 52, he saw this as possibly his last big adventure. He was gone for a month, my mother believing that he was in London. They kept in touch but he never revealed his true whereabouts until the operation was over and my mother remained blissfully unaware that he was not in fact in Pall Mall.

The author Graham Greene and the Colombian novelist *Gabriel Garcia Marquez*, both, sympathisers of the Marxists' cause, contacted my father through intermediaries and offered him valuable advice on how to negotiate with Farabundo. My father described his meeting with Marquez in a Mexico City hotel as one of the most interesting of his career. They talked not only of politics but about Mexico, South America and literature.

The bank contracted body guards through a company called Control Risks to shadow my father whilst he was in San Salvador. The three operatives were former Special Forces soldiers who had served in the SAS. They accompanied him as he drove around the city picking up messages and communications left in dead drops by Farabundo and watched his every move. It was a tense, exciting time, and although the two bank employees were eventually released, my Father had to leave San Salvador suddenly one morning, when Control Risks intercepted a communiqué from a splinter group of Farabundo which outlined a plan to kidnap him on his way to a dead drop. He remained in close contact with his minders, having spent hours with them cooped up in hotel rooms and down-town bars in the seedier parts of San Salvador.

There were other interesting trips. In 1975 my father visited Cuba and met *Fidel Castro* in an effort to interest the Cuban government in opening a branch of the bank in Havana. He reported that Castro had a wonderful sense of humour and he returned to Mexico with several boxes of cigars but nothing in the way of a deal.

In their retirement my parents continued to travel. A year before the First Gulf War they drove to Baghdad via Kurdistan to stay with friends and travelled to India and Oman.

Travelling therefore became a way of life for me from an early age. My earliest memories are of travelling in Mexico; to beaches on the Pacific. I remember aged two being terrified of a large pink crab in Zihuatanejo. During the holidays we explored the interior of the country, visiting hot springs and Aztec and Mayan ruins. One year we drove down to *Chiapas* and into the jungle and then up through *Yucatán*. Every two years we returned to the United Kingdom and toured England, Wales and Scotland in a Bedford van. After 10 years in Mexico, my father was posted to Venezuela. We made trips into the jungle - to *Colonia Tovar*, the eccentric German colony, where we ate sausages and sauerkraut, to the sound of chattering monkeys.

When we lived in Spain we explored the country extensively from Andorra and the Pyrenees to the Sierra Nevada and the Costa del Sol. One year we visited Communist Romania and the Ukraine.

By the time my father retired in 1986, my parents had moved house 23 times and lived in 8 countries. I recall a house we rented in Venezuela that came with a ferocious German shepherd. One afternoon it besieged me in my bedroom for several hours until I was released by the gardener. We found a coral snake coiled up in the back yard of another house. And then there was the house in Spain where the cesspit under the front lawn blew up one hot summer.

***

When I was nine years old, I went to boarding school in Sussex. Airports, planes and flying became a way of life. Aged 17, I travelled around Europe by train with three school friends and I spent my holidays from university organising mountaineering expeditions to the American Rockies and the Pyrenees. I walked across England with my father and sister, coast to coast and slogged my way over the Penine Way. When I graduated from St Andrews University in 1989, I spent a year teaching in Japan and returned to England a year later determined to travel as much as possible. After training as a journalist I set out to cycle China's Silk Road with three friends one of whom, David

George, had also lived in Mexico as a child and was a close family friend. The expedition was only partially successful. We failed in our attempt to cross the Pamir Mountains and reach the Pakistan Border, but we did see vast swathes of the country from Xian to the edge of the Taklamakan Desert and it whetted my appetite for further travels. Two years later, David and I returned to the Silk Road, this time approaching it from Islamabad at its western end. We spent five weeks cycling up the precipitous Karakoram Highway to the Khunjerab Pass, five thousand metres above sea level on the Chinese Border.

If the characteristics of a compulsive traveller are a constant urge for change and movement, then I am one. No sooner do I return from an expedition abroad and I begin planning the next. Sometimes these plans take months, even years to realise. First I buy all the travel literature I can on my chosen destination. I study maps and measure distances between points and repeat the names of exotic places.

A mixture of circumstances (call it fate) brought me back to Valle. Despite accounts that it had changed immensely in the 17 years since I was last there, I did return. A year of working as a free lance journalist yielded little except an ever decreasing bank balance. Although there were vague promises of interesting commissions, I had grown weary of life in London and longed to travel again. And then out of the blue, beckoning me back came the invitation. Nancy Blackmore was over in London from Mexico recruiting teachers for the school.

'I don't suppose Marcus would be interested in the job?' she asked my mother casually over tea one afternoon in May.

'I doubt he would be qualified for it. He's a journalist not a teacher, but I shall certainly mention it to him.'

Three months later I was on a plane bound for Mexico with a two year contract to work for *La Escuela Valle de Bravo*, 124 miles south west of Mexico City deep in the Sierra Madre Mountains. Behind me I had left no mortgage to pay and no fixed job. If things didn't work out I would return to the U.K in two years time. I had nothing to lose!

CHAPTER 14
LA COMIDA

We are riding through thick woods somewhere above *Avandaro*. The white waters of *La Vela de la Novia* cascade down into the lake below us. I can hear a woodpecker hammering against a tree. My legs are not long enough to reach the stirrups so my feet dangle over the sides of the saddle. *Paloma's* ears suddenly prick up. She's a dappled grey. She stops and begins pawing the ground with her hoof. *Chucho* has stopped in front of me. I can hear a faint rattling sound. And then I see what is making the noise. It's a rattlesnake coiled in the dust by the side of the trail.

***

Mark introduced me to *'El de tres dedos,'* a *taco* vendor who operated from a filthy side street next to the market. The Three Finger Wonder, as we translated his nick name, owned a stall with a yellow tarpaulin in *Callejon de las Monjas*. As his name suggests, Javier only had three fingers on his right hand. No one dared to ask him what had happened to the other two but watching him wield his meat cleaver as he chopped up thick pieces of steak on a wooden board was enough to feed a fertile imagination. The 'Wonder' in his name referred to his unbeatable tacos.

A community of stray dogs that feasted off the taco scraps in the gutter also inhabited Callejon de las Monjas. They reminded me of a group of schoolboys. There was the 'bully', with Rottweiler somewhere in his genes that always got the best pickings by growling and pushing the other dogs out of the way. Then there was the 'intellectual', a rather delicate looking Afghan hound, who I imagined wearing spectacles. He looked down his snout in a superior sort of way at the other dogs. And then there was the rest of the gang, an odd mixture of breeds, shapes and sizes that followed the bully and ignored the intellectual.

There were other taco vendors in the same alley but none as good as Three Fingers, who always had a queue at his stall. His lamb, pork and beef tacos were accompanied by copious amounts of coriander, fried onions and red pepper and only cost a couple of pesos each.

Another of my favourite eateries was the *Monarca* named after the Monarch butterfly. The Monarca was famous for its natural fruit juices and its *comida corrida* – a set menu which ran all day and cost 15 pesos for three courses and a drink.

The Monarca's proprietor was *Juvenal*, a former bank clerk. He was a large jovial man who always had something to talk about. At the Monarca, almost every fruit juice imaginable was on offer: orange, lemon, apple, prickly pear, carrot, passion fruit, raspberry, melon, papaya and even alfalfa. You name it, he had it!

It was the only restaurant in town that I frequented often enough to be offered my very own table as soon as I appeared in its large open doorway. Luis, the waiter and I would go through the same ritual. He would ask me what I wanted to drink and I would order a guava juice. I had many favourite dishes at the Monarca: pork in spicy green tomato sauce; breaded veal with avocado; spare ribs in chilli sauce; chicken with orange and sesame seeds and broccoli cakes in batter were just a few.

One afternoon in late October, Juvenal invited me to join him in business. He took a break from the kitchen and came to chat to me.

'*Don* Marcus, do your parents in Britain have a garage? It's simple. This is what we do. You put up a sign saying 'Monarca II – cheap meals and fruit juices.' You could do it from your garage like we do here in Mexico. I will handle the export of fruit from Mexico twice a week. All you need is a *liquadora* and some plates, cutlery and glasses. How about it?'

Another good place for tacos was *La Taquería de Don Rafael*, off the square. It was one up on 'Three Fingers' in having chairs, tables and a roof, a distinct advantage in the rainy season, but the tacos were not quite as spicy and were missing that little something. Mark and I nicknamed Rafael, Canon Nostrils. This was not only due to their extraordinary diameter, but also because he had a tendency to tilt his head backwards as if he were aiming at you, whilst taking the order.

Canon Nostrils served a delicious sauce, rich in chilli and avocado.

I shall never forget the evening when some colleagues and I had gone to Rafael's for tacos. Lying across a neighbouring table were two unconscious drunks, their empty glasses of beer still clutched lightly in their hands. I recognised one of them. He was the butcher who worked next door. I had seen him earlier in the day cutting up a sheep's carcass.

We were just finishing our meal when the butcher suddenly stood up. He shook his head a couple of times, took a few tentative steps and then fell forward onto the table which collapsed under his weight, taking his companion with him. The two men lay in a heap on the floor groaning with green sauce running through their hair and down their faces.

The two were obviously regulars at Rafael's, since the owner ignored them completely even though they had broken a set of chairs and a table.

The *Girasol,* in front of the Church of San Francisco had old sepia photographs of Valle hanging on mustard coloured walls and chunky pine tables and chairs. It was a warm, welcoming place to sit with a book over a steaming cup of *cafe de olla* on a rainy afternoon. Its owner was Patti Muller. She was tall with blonde hair and heavy Germanic features.

'I'm Mexican,' she explained, 'which means I don't really know where I am from. My great grandfather was Lebanese, my father was born here and my mother's family were from Germany, via Latvia!'

The Girasol served wonderful soups and freshly made pizzas and cakes.

***

It was Patti's brother who had organised the Avandaro Rock Festival. In September 1971, two years after Woodstock, young middle class Mexicans celebrated their own home-grown rock festival. No one could have imagined that what was originally conceived of as a post car rally party, would turn into the biggest rock event that Latin America had witnessed. For several years young Mexicans from the city had been coming to Valle to rally cars and motorcycles in the pine forest above Valle. On this particular occasion, the 11th of September, due to the proximity of the National Festival of Independence on the 15th, the rally organisers had planned an extra celebration. Although the event was much publicised in Mexico City, the organisers estimated that a maximum number of 5,000 people would attend, given that September was still the rainy season and that the event was to be held in the open air. Although entry to the event was for ticket holders only, access to the concert was not controlled. By the eve of the 10th September 15,000 fans had assembled in Avandaro all anxious to experience an unforgettable night of rock and roll. The inhabitants of Valle could not believe their eyes and there was a feeling of widespread panic that the revellers would rampage through the town destroying property and generally disrupting the quiet life of the town. Many shopkeepers fearing the worst closed early. Soon supplies of food and water began to run out. The following day the 11th of September, the rain which had begun falling the previous night, showed no sign of stopping. But nothing it seemed could dampen the enthusiasm of the partygoers who now numbering over 29,000, danced took drugs, had sex and got drunk as if there was no tomorrow. By the night of the 12th of September, driven by hunger, exhaustion and cold the revellers began to drift home, many of them embarking on a 150 mile walk back to Mexico City. To assist with the evacuation, The Federal District Department sent 300 buses along with supplies of food and warm clothing and by Independence Day most of the rock and rollers had left. But Valle could never be the same again. The festival was a milestone in local history, putting it on the map for a whole new generation, many of whom, later in life like Patti herself came back to live in the town as artists, writers or just to 'bum' in the hippie tradition of 'hanging out.

***

Next door to the cinema was *El Dorado* owned by *Andres* – the macho man as he liked to call himself. Here they served steaks with French fries and huge salads. Andres liked to chat.

'So when are we going out looking for girls?' he asked me casually one evening.

'What exactly do you mean?' I replied.

LA COMIDA

'I mean it's good for a man to get laid. All you have to do is look around, see a girl that you like and take her. Come on man, loosen up a little!'

As he was speaking, I spotted a pretty young woman in the kitchen with a baby in her arms.

'Is she your wife, by any chance?' I asked him.

'Yeah, so what? I don't need her approval if I want to go with another woman,' Andres said, laughing.

'How would you feel if she slept with another man?'

The smile left Andres' face and he scowled. 'How would I feel if I knew my wife was screwing another guy? I'll tell you, I'd kill him first and then her!'

'Do most Mexican men think like you?' I asked jokingly.

'Sure we do – we're Latinos, we are hot blooded and passionate not like you frigid gringos!'

'Then there is quite a chance that there are some angry husbands out there who wouldn't mind seeing you dead, for sleeping with their wives.'

Andres thought for a moment and then the smile returned to his face.

'True,' he said, 'that's very logical, but who gives a shit, they can come and get me and take their chances.' And with that he stood up, and thrusting out his pelvis, he clutched his crotch in one hand and strutted back to the kitchen.

Andres always had grandiose plans that never came to anything.

'I'm off to Italy next week,' he announced when I stopped by for a snack of *quesadillas*.

'I'm going to work as a chauffeur for this rich guy in Milan; you'll see I'll come back a rich man too!'

'How did you get the job?'

'My cousin is out there and suggested I join him. He says the women are fabulous and that they love Mexican men.'

'Will your wife be working there too?'

'No she doesn't want to go. She and the kid can stay here for all I care. They are not going to stand in the way of me and success.'

A month later I returned to El Dorado to find Andres at his usual place behind the griddle cooking steaks.

'What happened to Italy?' I asked him.

'Italy? I changed my mind, my cousin says the food is crap – but maybe I'll go next year.' And he quickly changed the subject.

'So when are you and I going to go out for some *putitas*?'

***

Nancy was a true Christian and genuinely believed in 'loving her neighbour,' so when she announced over lunch one day that she wanted to feed the poorest *barrio* in the town, I was not at all surprised.

'There are people in Valle who wake up in the morning and go to bed at night without having eaten one good meal and I propose doing something about it,' she said.

Robert, who was the calm voice of reason in the marriage applauded Nancy's resolve to help the poor but suggested that Valle might not be the best place to start this admirable project.

'I agree that there is poverty here, certainly by our standards, but no one is starving. Yes there are people living in shacks without proper sanitation and their children run about in the mud and dust in bare feet but many of the poorest at least own a bit of land where they can grow some maize for tortillas and keep a few chickens.'

But Nancy was adamant and would not brook any opposition to her plans of setting up a mobile kitchen to service Valle's poorest communities. A month later when sufficient funds had been raised and Nancy had recruited a small army of volunteers, Mark and I drove up the muddy cobbled road to *San Mateo* for the opening of the mobile kitchen.

There had been a great deal of discussion about where exactly to start the project. Valle had various shanties, all of which merited Nancy's help but it was agreed that it would be a mistake to spread ourselves too thinly and end up helping no one. We had limited resources and it was therefore decided to concentrate on one neighbourhood. *Mario*, the Blackmores' gardener, suggested San Mateo. He had relatives there and said we would be well received.

As Mark drove the battered Beetle up the hill we could smell Nancy's sausage and kidney stew which was perched precariously on the back seat. There was also a mountain of hot fresh tortillas and a pot of *frijoles*; enough to feed a small army.

My first impression of the hamlet was how neat and modern everything looked. There was a small primary school with a basketball court, a chapel and a medical centre. The houses, though mostly consisting of one or two rooms, looked well maintained and clean. We parked the car, and waited for Nancy who was following behind. Presently she arrived with Mario at the steering wheel of the old Ford. Nancy directed us to carry the food to the school yard where Mario had already set up some trestle tables.

'Those kids over there look pretty overweight to me,' Mark said cynically, pointing to two boys of about 11 years of age who were shooting baskets. He quickly grabbed a tortilla and dipped it into the gravy. Soon the whole village had gathered and were queuing up in an orderly manner. Nancy had organised the operation meticulously. There were enough plastic bowls and spoons to feed the entire village.

Mark and I ladled out the food whilst Nancy oversaw the whole proceeding making sure that the children of village ate first, followed by the elderly. We had been serving for about 20 minutes when a woman arrived at the table rubbing her red swollen eyes. On seeing her, Nancy turned to Mark and said:

'I think the old dear has been moved to tears by what we have done here today.'

A few moments later when Nancy had turned to hand a man some tortillas, Mark whispered to me:

'That woman wasn't crying! She has conjunctivitis!'

We must have fed 80 people that afternoon; some of them even came back for second helpings which amused Mark.

'They've never seen anything like it,' he said laughing. 'Free food like this; it's a greedy boy's paradise, but I honestly don't think any of these people really need it, do you?' and he pointed at a young man sitting down on the basketball court.

'He came back for seconds and now he's got himself a hamburger from somewhere. Do you think he's starving?'

I had to agree. There was no one in San Mateo that afternoon that looked remotely malnourished. The money for the food kitchen might have been better spent on providing training or workshops for some of the young unemployed men of the village; but no one had the heart to tell Nancy this.

CHAPTER 15

LA CANTINA

Las Adas is a hotel built in the style of a white-washed Moroccan village on the Pacific. It has just opened and dad has been invited to stay for a week. We sleep in a chalet covered in orange and purple bougainvillea. There are flowers on the table when we open the door and a large bowl of fruit. There's no one on the beach and the sand is hot and white and reminds me of talcum powder. In the evening a Mariachi band plays. We are the only guests. At night I am sick. Mum says I probably ate too much fruit.

***

The school day began at eight o'clock and finished at two. I volunteered for the morning duty which involved meeting the children at the school gates as they were dropped off. The approach to the school was up a steep rutted dirt road and depending on the season it was either a muddy mire or a cloud of powdery dust, both creating hazardous conditions for young children and lots of morning traffic.

Being new to the school, the morning duty provided me with an opportunity to get to know the children and their parents early on in the term. Mondays always began with a formal assembly where the Mexican flag was paraded and everyone was obliged to sing the state and national anthems before the first class of the morning. Being a bilingual school, three of the six lessons were in English and three in Spanish with a 40 minute break at midday.

I knew immediately I stepped through the gates that this was a happy, well run school. You could see it on the children's faces when they arrived in the morning, the smiles, the cheerful greetings – the way they went about the school, enjoyed their lessons and played at break time. Of course there were incidents, and fights and the odd rogue who would disappear to smoke or play truant but these were so few that they stood out as aberrations from the usual day to day life of the school. I recall one boy putting staples in

LA CANTINA

a teacher's mug of coffee: but his father was a drug dealer and he was brought up by his ageing grandmother.

When school ended and it wasn't raining I would walk into town and lunch in the market taking the set menu that cost less than three pounds. Twice a week I stayed on at school to run a hockey and camp craft club for an hour but the rest of the afternoon and the evenings were mine.

Often I would meet up with Mark to play pool. There must have been five pool halls in Valle and that didn't include many of the hotels that had tables in their bars.

Cantinas were dimly lit, 'men only' establishments, where youths in sweaty vests and tilted baseball caps gathered to combat with cue, chalk and pool balls on tables with torn, faded green baize. In the corners and around the walls sat the onlookers: brooding drunks in cowboy hats with scarred faces and bulging bellies. Mark and I were the only gringos that frequented these places, and often play would cease when we appeared through the swinging doors and everyone would look up as if a poncho clad Clint Eastwood had silently stepped inside. We would greet everyone collectively and someone would grunt back and we would order a round of beers, pay for a table, and select our cues and then we would play for an hour or two and Mark would always win.

After twenty minutes, when it was clear we weren't going to bother anyone, a few fellow players would gather around to watch Mark finish me off. No one would say as much, but you knew they admired and respected his skill; the way he could curve the ball or put back spin on it or pot a ball from an unlikely angle. You knew too that some of them were itching to challenge him to a game, but were afraid to do so in front of their peers in case they didn't win and lost face. There was always that invisible barrier where we were on the outside looking in, tolerated but never quite accepted.

***

It was in a cantina not two blocks away from my house that *Juan Ramirez* was shot. Juan was a big man with sirloin steak hands and legs as thick as tree trunks. He had a wild bushy moustache and a lively open face. Juan lived on a *ranchito* in the

LA CANTINA

mountains some 12 miles outside Valle. He came to town to sell wood and maize but mainly to drink in his favourite bar. He was known for his volatile temper, his love of Tequila and for his endless bragging and *machismo*.

'No one will ever get the better of me,' he would say leaning against the bar and swilling down shots. 'No drug dealer, no city hotshot and no fucking gringo. I tell you,' he went on thumping the surface of the bar with his clenched fist, 'I'll shoot anyone who tries to get the better of me!'

One morning two weeks later, Juan caught the seven o'clock bus to Mexico City. He had gone to visit his brother who lived near the airport and worked as a mechanic. By the time the bus reached Toluca, Juan was already drunk and abusive. The bus driver threatened to call the *judiciales* and have him thrown off if he didn't calm down.

When the bus arrived in Mexico City, Juan removed a wodge of 100 peso bills from his wallet and counting them in full view of the crowded terminal, flagged down a taxi and asked to be taken to *Hangares*. As they drove through the heavy morning traffic the combined effects of the alcohol and the capital's altitude soon had Juan fast asleep and snoring in the back of the taxi, his worn leather wallet bulging with bills held lightly between his fingers and a small Smith and Wesson revolver tucked into his trousers.

For the foolish taxi driver, the temptation to rob the man was too great to resist. Noticing that Juan was asleep, he took a detour through some quiet backstreets. He stopped the car, leaned gently over the seat and took the wallet from Juan's fingers. He then went for the gun with a smooth walnut handle, but Juan woke up and with his right hand he instinctively grabbed the gun, pulled it from under his belt and fired. Two shots rang out in the empty quiet street. The first shattered the windscreen, the second went through the taxi driver's forehead, forcing him back onto the steering wheel and then onto the passenger seat. A thin tickle of blood ran through his hair from a large hole in the back of his head.

Juan was still very drunk and he moved slowly. He fumbled for his wallet and tucked the gun back into his belt. Getting out of the car he weaved his way down to busy *Viaducto*. He was oblivious to the blood on his face and the large red stain on his shirt.

A week later, Juan was back in Valle boasting once again in *La Cantina Santa Rosa*. 'You know my friend, that *pendejo* asshole had it coming to him,' he said, laughing and slapping his enormous thigh. 'No one gets the better of me!'

Minutes before, a police car silently came to a halt outside the cantina. The only warning of its approach had been the reflection of its blue and red lights in the bar window, but Juan was too drunk to notice. The barmaid disappeared into the kitchen. The two young men wearing hooded tops and tattered jeans, who had been playing pool, hastily left the cantina. A policeman invisible to those inside announced through a megaphone that they had come for Juan Ramirez. 'Don't try anything stupid,' warned the officer in charge. But Juan Ramirez was not about to let anyone get the better of him. First a beer bottle and then a chair crashed through the window. And then Juan appeared stumbling through the cantina's swinging doors, waving his revolver, a bull of a man, flushed red with rage and too much *mescal*. Crouching behind the squad car, a police marksman fired a single shot from a range of four metres that passed straight between Juan's eyes. He reeled back through the cantina's doors and crashed to the ground. The charge was noted in a neat black pad attached to the officer's belt: 'resisting arrest.'

CHAPTER 16

EL DIA DE LOS MUERTOS

It's The Day of the Dead today. Mum has bought us little sugar skulls decorated with sequins to have for pudding. There was a piñata at school in the shape of a skeleton. We each took it in turns to hit it with a broom stick. *Pepe* broke it open and sweets, peanuts and fruit came tumbling out. A fat boy called *Javier* pushed me out of the way so that he could get more sweets. Mrs Roth, the teacher gave me a Hershey Bar instead.

***

Jorge Balzaretti owed money to everyone in Valle. His four children, always immaculately dressed in the latest clothes from Benetton, all attended La Escuela Valle de Bravo, where their school fees had not been paid in two years.

Alejandra Gerrard allowed them to stay on for sentimental reasons. They and their ongoing debts had become part of the school's history. The eldest son, *Juan Claudio* had been one of the school's first pupils and now three years on was about to graduate to *secundaria*. The family's squabbles and crises, the kids playing truant and never completing their homework and Jorge's termly trips up to the school to reassure the administrator that a big cheque was on its way were the few constants in both the school's and Vallle's dynamic and ever changing life. Shops would open and close two months later; people would move to Valle and others would leave, the school prospered one year and took a step back the next, but *Jorge Balzaretti* with his debts and anarchic family never changed.

Jorge owned a lavish restaurant and bar a stone's throw away from the square, where Valle's community of ageing, hippie hang glider pilots hung out to play pool, drink rum and discuss the highs and lows of their most recent flying exploits. In Valle you could always distinguish the pilots from any other sporting fraternity. The sailors were a mixed group of ages, professions and appearances, but the fliers all looked the same: tanned, ear-ringed, pony-tailed, scruffy and permanently 'high.'

On the eve of *El Dia de los Muertos*, All Souls – I had met a friend for a drink at Balzaretti's. We played some frames of pool, and drank some beers and then moved to the bar and ordered *Margaritas*. Before long, our bar tab had extended to a dozen beers and several cocktails and I had completely forgotten that within six hours I was supposed to be meeting Mark and two others to climb *El Nevado de Toluca*. I stumbled out of the bar at one o'clock in the morning and somehow got home, though I do not recall how. What I do remember was the hammering on my door at seven o'clock the following morning and shouts from the street below.

'Marcus, get up; we know you are in there!' shouted Mark. With a heavy hangover, I dragged myself out of bed, had a quick shower and gathered up my ice axe, crampons and other items of equipment into my rucksack. With my bootlaces still undone and my shirt unbuttoned, I opened the gate to find Mark standing with Josefina's ladder in his hands and a grin on his face.

'I was just about to climb through your window and give you the fright of your life.'

El Nevado de Toluca at 15,300 feet, towers over the State of Mexico. Resembling a boiled egg with its top sliced off, it casts a shadow over the sierra. As we twisted and turned up the serpentine road, I sat squashed in the back of the Beetle, my head buried in a cushion in an attempt to sleep off the effects of a heavy night of drinking.

After two hours, we stopped at a roadside shack that passed for a restaurant. This marked the turn-off for the volcano. Whilst Mark, Rocio and Carlos ordered tacos and *atole*, I dashed for a patch of greenery behind the shack where I was violently sick. I felt much better after vomiting, but still not ready for spicy tacos and thick, stringy Oaxaca cheese. The most I could manage was a bottle of Pepsi that did something to settle my stomach.

The others observed me with mild amusement as they crammed platefuls of food into their mouths. A few minutes later we were off again onto the single-track of shale that led 10 miles to the climbers' bivouac. It was a beautifully clear morning but when we got out at 10,000 feet, the air was thin and chilly.

We parked the car at the mountain refuge and geared up. Both Rocio and Carlos were experienced mountaineers and had climbed all Mexico's volcanoes and various Andean peaks. Mark had never been up a mountain in his life.

There was nothing technical about the scramble to the crater rim, but there was no path and we slipped constantly on the loose scree and progress was slow. Mark soon began to feel the effects of the altitude. He took one or two steps at a time, his head down, taking long breaks to catch his breath whilst we watched for further symptoms of mountain sickness.

Eventually we reached the rocky saddle on the crater rim where we sat to admire the view. Below us was Toluca beneath a layer of brown greasy smog. In the distance the white conical summits of *Popo* and *El Pico de Orizaba* (Mexico's highest mountain) could be seen piercing the deep blue sky. The Crater Lake was now 3,000 feet below us at the bottom of a precipice. We watched as a party of climbers began their ascent. They looked like ants among the moraine and boulder fields. We pressed on to the elusive summit, scrambling from one rocky shelf to another. After a further 30 minutes of climbing we reached the top and sat panting in the cold air looking down on what seemed like the whole of Mexico.

The descent took no time at all. We chose a direct route down, abseiling and traversing the mountain's steep western face until we reached the crater rim. From there, we slid and jumped down 1000 feet of sand and cinder to the lake. Among the prickly pears and volcanic rock we picnicked on steak sandwiches, apples and chocolate and basked in the early evening sun.

***

Back in Valle, the Day of the Dead was being celebrated. The first and second of November are of particular significance in Mexico, combining the ancient pagan cult of *Mictlantecutli*, the Aztec Lord of the Underworld, with the Christian observance of All Souls Day. It's a colourful tradition and one that breaks many of the taboos concerning death felt elsewhere in the world. The week leading up to El Dia de los Muertos was one of expectation as families prepared to welcome back the souls and spirits of their dearly departed. Vallesanos built altars to their dead, adorning them with photographs of their loved ones and particular items of memorabilia along with food and drink.

Cake shops and bakeries sold icing sugar skulls (with eyes of shiny paper) for children to eat. Skeleton images were everywhere and the streets were decked out in *papel picado* – colourful bunting made out of tissue paper with skeleton and skull shapes cut out of it. Shops and roadside stalls sold model skeletons playing football, smoking and drinking; skeleton matadors, skeletons driving cars and playing pool. They reminded me of the figures in Hieronymus Bosch's painting 'The Harrowing of Hell,' though these characters adorning stalls and shop windows were comical and colourful. The mood on The Day of the Dead, far from being morbid or gloomy, was one of *fiesta* as families gathered at twilight in the cemeteries to lay marigolds and light candles on their relatives' graves. They brought food and drink and sat on blankets and rush mats late into the night talking and laughing.

Ignacio, Josefina's Mazahua gardener explained to me what the festival was all about:

'Death is not a stranger to us. We grow up and see it all the time. I saw my little brother die of dysentery when I was ten years old. We buried my grandparents here in the graveyard of Santa Maria. Death to us is as familiar as birth.'

I had never seen a person dying, much less a corpse. Death for me was something remote; the body counts in celluloid film. When real people died, they were rushed away in ambulances with tinted windows or wrapped in body bags. People I knew never joked about death.

Rocio put it this way: 'For the pre-Hispanic people of Mexico, death was terrifying and inexplicable. The only way to diminish its terror was to joke about it, to caricature it, to rationalise it – even to welcome and celebrate it!'

I was reminded of a scene from the film 'Patch Adams' in which Robin Williams plays an irreverend doctor who tries to cheer up a terminally ill patient by bombarding him with a series of euphemisms for death and dying: 'Dirt nap, stiff, expired, terminated, kicked the bucket, fertilizer, rubbed out...' he reels off a whole list until the poor man is shaking with laughter and finally comes to terms with what is happening to him.

⁂

CHAPTER 17

LAS MARIPOSAS

We have come to *Santo Tomas de los Platanos* to see Halley's Comet passing. The village is perched high up on a cliff where the skies are wide and full of stars. We are sitting in the *zocalo*. Hundreds of people have gathered to see the comet. There are taco vendors and old women cooking *tamales* and selling atole under the colonnades. I fall asleep after midnight just before the comet passes.

***

I rose early and locking my wooden gate behind me, I walked towards the square passing Joaquin, the wood seller. *Francisco* was fanning his charcoal stove and preparing tacos under the porticos. A tortilla vendor was conducting brisk business, steam rising from a large pile of flat maize breads wrapped in a linen cloth. Then the bells tolled and widows in black scurried towards Santa Maria church.

It was Sunday morning so I stopped at the Monarca for a leisurely breakfast. Juvenal was squeezing oranges into a jug in the open doorway. 'So, Don Marcos how is the world today?' he gleamed, 'Your usual table?'

He gestured me to a corner from where I could observe the comings and goings of the town's busiest street. Luis, the thin waiter with a wispy moustache approached.

'She left me on Friday for another man, Don Marcos,' he lamented, picking up the threads of a previous conversation.

'Her father said that I am not rich enough and just the son of a pig farmer.' I tried consoling him but he was called away.

I ordered crispy bacon, ranch style eggs and chilli sauce. Juvenal's little restaurant began filling up. I spotted the barber. He was complaining about the postal service.

'That letter from my sister in San Diego has still not arrived. The post office is full of crooks,' he said chewing on a toothpick. The police *sargento* sitting at the bar ordered a milkshake.

After breakfast I headed for the market. Lupita was gossiping with a fellow fruit seller. She saw me approaching and began flirting.

'It's the gringo,' she shouted.

'Have you come to ask for my hand in marriage?' she shrieked.

Her stall was a riot of colour and shape: bright orange papayas, rich green *chayotes*, avocados, bushels of pungent coriander and wormwood, strings of chillies and peppers and bags of hibiscus petals. I bought some oranges and two large pineapples and chatted to Lupita.

'They shot another drug-dealer in the cantina in Temascaltepec yesterday,' she said nonchalantly.

Outside, mass was ending. As I made my way home I passed *Cajetas*, the town's tramp. No one knew his real name, or where he came from. It was said he appeared one day in 1961. There were rumours that he had been a bandit; that he had ridden with the notorious *Jimenez* brothers who had terrorised the lawless roads of Guerrero state. Now he never spoke, he just mumbled and dressed himself in clothes stolen from people's washing lines. We exchanged glances and he shuffled on.

Leaving my shopping at home, I decided to go for a ride. I found *Jesus* with his string of horses down by the lake and paid him for two hours. I saddled *Relampago*, a beautiful dappled grey, and we set off towards the hills descending first towards the *Avandaro River*. The horses picked their way gingerly through the foaming waters and then up the steep wooded slopes between pine and jacaranda trees. We rode in silence. A woodpecker hammered against a branch, a curlew's shrill call echoed through the forest. After half an hour we emerged out onto open pasture spotted with poppies and *magueys*. A crop of dried maize rattled in the warm breeze.

Presently we arrived at the hamlet of *San Jose*. Three barefooted *Otomi* girls dressed in brightly coloured petticoats ran out to meet us.

'Can we have a peso for a *refresco*,' they shouted.

At the village shop we dismounted and tethered the horses to a post. I bought the girls a coke each and two cold beers for Jesus and me. We sat on the porch and chatted. Below us in the distance we could see Valle and the lake shimmering in the early afternoon. A Monarch butterfly landed delicately on my knee and opened its orange spotted wings.

'My people call them daughters of the sun,' said Jesus wistfully. 'They are the bringers of peace and light, but soon they will migrate northwards.'

***

For a month people in Valle had been expecting the arrival of the Monarch butterfly. The previous year Monarchs had been spotted near *Los Saucos*, just outside Toluca. Conservationists had put up roadblocks allowing traffic through at a snail's pace whilst flocks of the delicate orange and black butterfly fluttered across the highway on their way to the forests of Michoacan. But this year none had been seen. Some said it was the frost; the weather had been too cold on account of *El Niño*. So I decided to drive up to Michoacan to see them and teamed up with a group of Conservationists who were heading to Michoacan.

Getting to *Sanctuario Roasrio* was a small adventure. We drove out of Valle heading west towards the town of *Zitacuaro* on the state border. After a three hour drive through lush hills we arrived at the town of *Ocampo,* a centre for honey and rapeseed oil. Leaving the car parked just outside the town, we chartered a local driver with a pickup truck for the next stage of the journey. For an hour we drove off-road on a dirt track, fording several rivers, deep into the mountains. It was early November and as we drove steadily higher into cloud forest the temperature plummeted and we struggled to keep warm, squatting in the back of the pickup truck. After a buttock numbing ride we drove into a clearing where there was a forest ranger's post and some taco stands. We were now at 11,000 feet above sea level and the muddy ground had frozen into iron-hard furrows.

As we stood stomping the ground and rubbing our hands in an effort to keep warm, we noticed that there was an abundance of butterflies littering the path like colourful sweet wrappers, their wings twitching almost imperceptibly. And then, looking up, the groves shifted and we realised that what was weighing their branches down were not leaves but thousands of butterflies.

***

Every year a unique pattern of migration takes place. Millions of Monarch butterflies leave their North American habitat and fly 3,000 miles to a few specific sites in the woods of Central Mexico.

The brief four month life of a Monarch begins on the underside of a milkweed leaf in the forests of Eastern Canada. Five days after mating, the female lays her eggs and within 30 days the metamorphosis from larvae to adult butterfly is complete. As autumn approaches, hormonal changes awaken the instinct to migrate and the butterflies accumulate vital fats which will fuel them on their epic flight south.

Whilst the Monarchs are preparing for their journey, thousands of miles away on the forested slopes of the Sierra Madre, equally significant changes are occurring. After more than five months of rain, hundreds of wild flowers begin to blossom in upland meadows and these will provide a ready source of nectar and nourishment for the butterflies when they arrive after their exhausting flight.

Why the Monarch butterfly returns to Mexico every autumn remains an enigma. What is equally baffling is that different generations of butterfly are capable of locating exactly the same sites year after year. Some experts believe that the butterflies use the earth's magnetic fields to navigate. Although millions of Monarchs migrate every year, there appears to be no formal social grouping along the way. Each butterfly makes the 3,000 mile journey unaided, flying alone for up to six hours a day.

When the butterflies finally arrive in the Sierra Madre in November, their recovery is remarkably quick. Gorging themselves on nectar they fly to the higher elevation of the *oyamel* forests after just two or three days. Here grouping in trees in numbers of up to 100,000 they spend the winter months in semi-dormancy. With the coming of the spring equinox their reproductive organs develop and the mating season takes place. This process coincides with the appearance of spring flowers on which the butterflies feed in preparation for their flight northwards.

***

As midday approached and light began to penetrate the dark woods, the dormant butterflies opened their wings to the heat. And then suddenly and very briefly we were treated to a spectacular display as the air filled with the sight and sound of millions of orange wings flashing like tongues of fire among the trees.

CHAPTER 18

HACIA LAS MONTAÑAS

At school today, a boy called *Carlos* called me a girl because I was wearing Clark's sandals. I hit him with my lunch box. There was blood on his face. The teacher told me off and said she would have to speak to my mother. I told her that English boys wore sandals.

***

It was the beginning of the dry season and to celebrate I decided to set off on my mountain bike into the hills. It was Friday afternoon and after school I returned home, ate a quick lunch, packed a few provisions into my rucksack and started out. My destination was *Ixtapan del Oro,* once a prosperous gold mine set in a remote valley.

I cycled out of Valle heading west around the lake and then down a narrow ravine to the town of *Colorines* known for its brothels. I skirted the town and took a minor road to a small hamlet where I asked for directions.

'I wouldn't take that road if I were you,' replied the old man. He looked at me through bloodshot, jaundiced eyes. 'It's 40 miles of tortuous bends and there is hardly enough room for a car,' he added rolling a thin piece of sugar cane from one side of his mouth to the other.

Looking at the map, I had to agree that the road looked perilous. It resembled a drawing I had once seen in a biology book of a rodent's intestines. There were so many twists and turns in the track that it looked as if the path might even double back upon itself.

I thanked the man for his concern and pedalled on. After cycling for 20 minutes I passed some corrugated iron shacks that marked the end of the tarmac and the beginning of the *terrazeria*. A group of grubby children guzzling cans of coke ran into the streets and waved. I waved back just as a large pig ran out of a corral and almost knocked me off my bike. I swerved just in time and pedalled hard. The kids shrieked with laughter as my tyres sent up a cloud of powder thin dust that covered me in grey.

The first 18 miles of the ride were deceptive. Far from being the hazardous road that I was expecting, it gently contoured a hillside of elephant grass and cornfields. Looking south west there were marvellous views of Santo Tomas de los Platanos, perched like a fortress on the side of a precipice across the valley from me. After another hour of cycling the track began to descend gradually through woods. I passed two boys who were resting by the roadside with a small herd of goats. They left the goats grazing on the grassy bank and ran after me cheering and whistling. They were the last people I saw for two blissful hours of cycling. I encountered none of the dangers that I had been warned of, though several roadside crosses were a reminder of potential disaster and at the bottom of one cliff I spotted the rusty, burnt out carcass of a bus.

Thirty miles of solitary cycling did not prepare me for the sight that confronted me as I rounded a hairpin bend in rapid descent. Picnicking on the side of a mountain was a group of about 20 men of all ages. They wore straw hats with black ribbons tied under their chins and their faces were flushed with alcohol. As I sped past they raised their hats and mescal jars in unison and shouted *'Andale* guerro!' I was reminded of *Velazquez'* bucolic painting *'Los Borrachos.'* They had chosen a good site. Beyond them rose range after range of hazy, blue mountains and the air smelt of wild flowers.

The first community that I came to was *Tutuapan*, just a string of houses along the track. The reaction I caused on cycling past was one of stupefaction. A group of young women dropped their washing and ran to stare at me. A child playing happily with a plastic football ran screaming to his mother's skirts. I felt like the black hatted baddie in a Spaghetti Western.

Ixtapan del Oro lay eight miles downhill from Tutuapan. Just outside the town I passed the ruins of the old gold mine tangled in vines and covered in moss and then a few hundred yards further on was the town across a shallow ford. Here I washed off the day's dust before cycling on to find accommodation for the night.

There was not much to see or do in Ixtapan apart from its waterfall and the ruined mine, but I had come for the journey and Ixtapan with its scent of guavas, its bougainvillea and the prospect of a cold beer seemed to me the perfect stop for a weary cyclist.

***

Carmelo owned a string of horses up in Avandaro which he rented out by the hour for 15 pesos. He was a stocky young man of about 21 years of age, with a thin moustache and a pock marked face. Whatever the weather, Carmelo always wore the same clothes: a short sleeved shirt, tight blue jeans and a pair of black slip on shoes with holes in their soles. But he was a born rider and there wasn't a horse in Valle that he couldn't break or master.

On returning from Ixtapan I met up with Carmelo. For a while he had been promising to take me to *El Divisadero*, a mountain some 15 miles out of Valle with wonderful views of the town and surrounding countryside. He said he would tell me the story of *Alberto Samano*, a Zapatista *bandido* from nearby Temascaltepec who had sacked Valle in 1912.

I rode *Conejo,* a black gelding with a tendency to bolt when startled, but after several rides, he had become accustomed to me. Leaving Avandaro, we rode along a forest trail that contoured the hills and passed through a small ranch where chickens ran about and dogs trotted out to meet us growling. Already two weeks into the dry season, there were flowers everywhere and the arid smell of dust and *ocote*.

Once the horses had settled into their stride and we were away from the dogs, Carmelo began his story.

'My great grandfather knew Samano. According to him Samano was a man of perverse inclinations, driven by the brutal appetites of greed and revenge. Samano started out as an independent miner in Temascaltepec and Ixtapan del Oro. Once a month he would bring a bag of ore to Valle where a certain friend called Señor *Boisson* minted fake coins. The two men would use the counterfeit money to buy and sell liquor on the black market in Toluca.

Before long, the circulation of the fake coins came to the notice of the state treasury and marshals were dispatched to investigate the source and arrest those involved in the operation. An anonymous tip-off led the marshals to Valle and to Boisson's workshop. Boisson, unlike his friend Samano, was considered a respectable and upright citizen of Valle. He also had friends in the mayor's office. Boisson convinced the marshals that the real villain was Samano. Moreover he confessed that though he had played a part in counterfeiting money, he had been coerced into doing so by Samano who had on more than one occasion threatened to kill him unless he co-operated.

The marshals accepted his story and Boisson was released. A few hours later, a warrant was out for Samano's arrest and Boisson himself had put up a reward of several hundred pesos for his apprehension. Samano was in Temascaltepec when he read the notice announcing the reward and he quickly fled on horseback through the mountains towards the neighbouring state of Guerrero with marshals and a cavalry brigade in pursuit.

Local legend has it that Samano took refuge in a cave deep in the mountains. As night fell he lit a small fire and huddled into one of the many recesses of the cavern. As the flames lit up the darkness, Samano was horrified to find that he was sharing the lair with a mountain lion that appeared to be asleep. The lion awoke during the night to hunt and to roam about in the mouth of the cave, but it never bothered Samano who remained vigilant by his fire, too afraid to sleep.

Meanwhile the posse on Samano's heels was led to the cave by the light of the fire. They had hardly ventured inside when they heard the lion roaring and saw the flash of its yellow eyes. Too terrified to investigate any further, the marshals concluded that not even a madman would seek refuge in such a place.

Over the following months Samano rode north evading capture by government troops until he eventually crossed the *Rio Grande* into the United States. There he laid low for several weeks working as a farm labourer until he decided it was safe enough to return to Mexico which he did travelling incognito with a group of peddlars.

It was between the years 1910 and 1912 that Samano's notoriety spread across the country as he made his audacious escape from one bank robbery to another. Ever since Boisson had betrayed him and he had been forced to make his desperate escape, he had been bent on revenge and so it was with this intent that he rode into Valle one rainy Saturday in the middle of September 1912. He quickly learned that Boisson now resided on a large *hacienda* in the neighbouring village of *San Gaspar* and so with a band of desperados he headed there with murder on his mind.

Neither Boisson nor his estate manager were able to put up any resistance so shocked were they by the sudden and unexpected appearance of the bandits. Samano's men proceeded to sack the farm burning buildings, killing livestock and plundering Boisson's considerable wealth. They were given strict orders not to harm Boisson himself who was to be left for Samano's own pleasure. His body was later found by government soldiers. He had been sodomised and horribly mutilated. That night other atrocities were committed by Samano and his bandits in and around the vicinity of Valle before he made his escape, once again an outlaw in every state.'

By now we had reached El Divisadero. We dismounted, tethered the horses to a tree and sat down in the soft pine needles. Below us, down a rocky slope, the waters of the lake lapped the shoreline. There were sailing boats out on the choppy waves and fishermen casting out their nets in the shallows. Carmelo propped his straw hat over his eyes and dozed. I watched as an army of black ants dragged a dead grasshopper into their nest.

'Very little is known about Samano's movements in the two years that followed,' Carmelo continued when we had mounted up and were making our way down to the water's edge, 'but early in 1914 he reappeared in Guatemala where he set up a small business running a cantina. For a while it seems, he left his life of crime and led an upright existence as an honest citizen of Guatemala City. But on Christmas Eve 1917, a terrible earthquake struck the country killing thousands of people. For Samano however, the disaster proved to be a bonanza. Emerging from the rubble of his ruined saloon and searching for the remains of his possessions, he stumbled upon an iron safe belonging to his neighbour. On forcing it open he discovered a small fortune of $50,000 and it gave him an idea.

He decided to steal his dead neighbour's identity and return to Mexico where he intended setting up business once again in *Tuxtla Gutierrez*.

Three days later he crossed the border at *Tapachula* where he spent the night in a local hotel splashing his new found wealth about on drink and whores. Unbeknown to him, a troop of 500 soldiers had arrived that morning in town to quell a local uprising. As one of the officers was eating his breakfast in the hotel, he recognized Samano and had him arrested shortly afterwards as he was leaving the hotel. On January 10th 1918 a court in Tuxtla sentenced Samano to death by firing squad. The following morning, he was taken from his cell and shot. He was buried in a pauper's grave outside the city walls. A few moments before he was executed, Samano was asked if he had any final requests. He replied, 'No,' but he did have a confession to make. Some years before, whilst on the run from federal forces, he had taken refuge in a cave near Valle de Bravo. There he had hidden a large amount of gold, hoping one day to return for it.

As we reached the lake, Carmelo turned in his saddle and pointed up to some craggy cliffs above us.

'It is said that Samano hid his treasure somewhere up there,' and he concluded his story. 'But my great grandfather told my father that the treasure is said to be cursed by all the blood that Samano shed.'

༄

CHAPTER 19

EL CAMPAMENTO

Clint Smith's father is also called Clint. He's in the U.S. navy and little Clint showed me his uniform hanging in the wardrobe. It's black with brass buttons and epaulettes. He also has a black and white gold braided peak cap. The girls are playing in the sitting room. Mrs Smith calls for Fiona. Fiona gets up quickly and then there's shattered glass and blood everywhere. Fiona is crying and her face and hands are red. A breeze comes through where the broken French doors used to be.

***

I met Hans Klost through the school. His daughter, Susanna was in my class and when she heard that I was looking for a suitable campsite for the fifth year camp, she said she would speak to her father.

Two days later Hans introduced himself. He was a large man with glasses and several days' growth of grey stubble. He spoke English fluently which surprised me since Susanna was dark skinned and could barely speak the language.

'You speak English well,' I said shaking his hand.

'That's because I'm Canadian,' he said smiling. 'I speak French too – and Spanish, my wife, Citlali, is Otomi. I hear you are looking for a campsite,' he went on, 'I've got the perfect place. It's half way up the mountain on a piece of flat ground between two paths. It's got its own spring and there are some rocks nearby that would be good for climbing on. How about you and Mark come up this Sunday? I'll show you around and then you can come back to the cabin for a meal?'

***

Hans' cabin was in the woods above Avandaro. His wife, Citlali, opened the door. She was a handsome, dark woman and spoke Spanish in lilting tones. She invited us in and fetched two cold beers from the kitchen. Presently Hans joined us. He was dressed in a heavy leather apron and was covered in sawdust.

'Bring your beers and I'll take you up there,' he said grabbing an old knapsack into which he threw a knife and a long *chorizo*. Outside in a yard were some carpentry workshops and tool sheds. An old Ford Galaxy lay rusting in the long grass and chickens pecked at seeds strewn along the drive way. We walked past some bee hives and then the path rose steeply through pines woods. After 20 minutes we reached a small opening in the woods where the ground was soft and ferny and a brook babbled between the trees.

'This is the place I had in mind,' said Hans panting. He took out a packet of tobacco, rolled a cigarette and lit it. 'You could pitch your tents here; you've got cold, clean water and masses of wood. What do you think of it?'

It was the perfect campsite. The climb up from the cabin would provide a challenge for the kids but it wasn't too far to haul up all the gear required for a night out in the woods.

***

Back at the cabin Hans opened a bottle of red wine. I was interested to know how a Canadian from Montreal had ended up married to an Otomi woman in Valle de Bravo.

'My parents were Mennonites and I grew up on a cheese commune in Chihuahua.' An image of old men with long beards clad in 19th century dress came to mind. The Klosts were true bohemians. Their cabin was filthy. There was dust and cobwebs everywhere and an eclectic mix of books, clothes, newspapers, art catalogues and dried out tubes of acrylic paint were piled up on every surface. Hans made a living as a carpenter but he was really an artist and had exhibited his paintings and sculptures all over the world. He made the most amazing objects out of wood which he warped and moulded in water into abstract shapes and forms.

He had been a hell raiser in his youth and a member of various anarchic, revolutionary groups in Canada.

'I suppose they would call me a terrorist nowadays,' he confessed. 'I did time for attempting to blow up a municipal building,' he said pouring out the wine.

***

EL CAMPAMENTO

The camp took place a month after the last of the rains. It was the middle of November and the countryside was beginning to dry out. There were wild flowers everywhere and the days were warm with pale blue skies.

At the end of classes on Friday afternoon, eight boys and four girls laden down with rucksacks piled into the back of two pickup trucks. The plan was to take them on an overnight camp and introduce them to basic camp-craft: tent pitching, fire building, outdoor cooking and mountain navigation. As we raced up the pot-holed road to Avandaro, children perched precariously on the sides of the trucks, I knew this sort of thing could never happen back in England. There were no seat belts – the kids were not even sitting on seats and an unexpected bump could send them flying over the sides or headlong into each other. But no one seemed concerned – least of all their parents. The children laughed and sang songs and let the wind blow through their hair.

Hans had arranged for a muleteer with two donkeys to carry all the heavy equipment and food up the mountain, so after saying goodbye to the parents, Mark, Rosa and I set off with the children up the hill. None of them had been on a real camp before, nor had they been exposed to outdoor pursuits or general camp craft. As we trudged up the hill, the more athletic among the group ran ahead taking the steep climb in their stride. The less fit complained ceaselessly about the weight of their packs, the heat and the walking. They munched through packets of sickly sweets and gulped down their water.

On arriving at the forest clearing, the children dumped their rucksacks and began collecting wood for the fire whilst we waited for the muleteer. After an hour they had amassed a huge pyre and were impatient to put up their tents but there was still no sign of the muleteer. Leaving the children with Mark and Rosa, I set off back down the hill to investigate. And then I saw him, running up waving his arms.

'There's been an accident Señor. One of the donkeys slipped and fell down the side of the hill and the other one took fright and ran off.'

We ran down the hill to see if we could locate the donkey that had fallen and found her a few minutes later grazing in a meadow surrounded by broken boxes containing packets of hot dogs, drinking chocolate, pasta and cartons of milk and the tents. The remainder of her cargo was strewn over the hillside. The other donkey that had been carrying some of the heavier climbing equipment was nowhere to be seen

It didn't take long to ferry all the kit up to the camp. We organised the children into a long chain and relayed everything up by hand but by nightfall the second donkey had still not returned.

***

The children were just getting into their sleeping bags and tents after a meal and ghost stories around the fire when a flash of forked lightning lit up the dark woods followed instantly by an almighty peel of thunder. Within seconds it was pouring with rain. The fire sizzled, the flames went down and minutes later it was just a smoking pile of wood and ash.

Mark, Rosa and I scrambled to get the food and bits of equipment that lay around the camp into our tent before reassuring the children that it was just a shower. We were after all well into the dry season. But the rain showed no signs of ceasing. There was more thunder and lightning and soon water was getting into the tents and soaking the sleeping bags. From within the tents we could hear the children laughing and giggling. We overheard a couple of them saying they hoped it rained all night. Others described it as 'A real adventure!' Soon the campsite was a large muddy pool and the rain was torrential. And then a lightning bolt hit a tree some 10 metres away from us and bits of bark and sparks flew into the air in a deafening explosion and some of the girls began to scream. Mark and I decided it was time to abandon the camp and get everyone off the hill as quickly as possible.

We instructed the children to dress and put on their waterproofs and warm clothing and to leave everything in the tents except their torches. Once outside we quickly assembled them into a line according to their ages with the youngest at the front and the eldest at the back. Mark took the rear and Rosa the front as I led the group off the hill. By the time we reached the trailhead and our escape route, the path was a running river sweeping down everything in its wake: branches, leaves and muddy banks – but we had no choice but to follow it. With the dim lights from our torches illuminating the dripping woods we slowly waded down the trail. In parts, the rain had collected in deep pools and the children plunged into cold water up to their waists. It was remarkable how they rose to the challenge and helped one another through the ordeal. For an hour and a half we crept down the mountain, the forests around us echoing with thunder. We encouraged the children to keep chatting to each other, knowing that this would distract them from the horrible night. By the time we reached the bottom of the hill it was 11 o'clock and the children were soaked to the skin, cold and exhausted but in surprisingly good spirits after an experience we could neither have planned nor forecast.

Hans had already called Alejandra who in turn had called all the parents and they were now waiting anxiously outside or in their cars. Citlali passed around steaming cups of atole, *pan dulce* and blankets and everyone huddled into the cabin to get out of the rain.

'I heard on the radio that this was a freak storm,' said Hans, chuckling. 'No one predicted it - it's El Niño's last act of revenge!'

***

Later in the week Nancy invited me for lunch. She wanted to hear all about the camp. 'That storm was the best thing that could have happened to some of those children,' she said as she served the golden syrup pudding.

'Experiences like that are character building and it clearly brought out the best in all of them. I wouldn't mind betting that you'll have other schools in Valle asking you to run camps for them too.'

Three days later, *Felipe Alfredo*, the headmaster of *El Instituto del Lago*, approached Mark and I as we sat over our comida corrida at the Monarca.

'We hear you run an excellent camp,' he said by way of an introduction. 'Perhaps you can organise one for us?'

CHAPTER 20

VENGANZA

Pancho returned with a gash in his head last night. Dad says he's been chasing cars again. He needed 15 stitches and the vet said he was lucky to be alive.

***

Pablo Ramos was the curator of *El Museo Pagaza*. His family had lived in and around Valle for generations so when I saw him in the *Michoacana* one afternoon, sipping a *cafe Americano* and reading his newspaper I pulled up a chair and asked him if he could tell me a bit about Valle's history. Inspired by Carmelo's tale I was particularly interested in finding out how the town had fared during the Revolution.

'Sure,' he said, 'just come to the museum preferably after four o'clock on any week day and I can show you the library and tell you what I know.'

Pablo must have been in his late sixties. He had brown eyes and a mop of grey hair. For many years he had taught History and Politics at Mexico's UNAM University but he had since retired to Valle to manage the museum.

Two days later I ambled across the road from the Culebra to meet Pablo. I found him in the storeroom filing old manuscripts and maps clad in a pair of corduroys and a cardigan.

'I thought that you might come today,' he said smiling. 'Give me a minute and I'll put on some coffee and we can chat and I can show you what resources we have.'

Pablo led me into the library and showed me the reference section. He took down one or two tomes and placed them delicately on the table.

'Have a look at these,' he said, '*Castillo* and *Piña* are probably the best authorities on that period, certainly where Valle is concerned, but if you want to hear some personal accounts of what life was like around that time, I've got one or two that might interest you.'

Presently a middle aged woman wearing round spectacles entered the room carrying a tray with coffee and a plate of *Maria* biscuits.

'I don't think you have met *Lourdes*, my secretary?' Pablo smiled and put his arm affectionately around the woman's shoulders. 'She also happens to be my wife.'

Lourdes laughed and extended her hand to me. '*Mucho gusto*,' she said. 'Any time you want to come to the library, just let me know and I will open it up for you. We live at number 5, San Sebastian Street.'

***

'If you will allow me,' Pablo continued, 'I would like to tell you a story that I think illustrates what life for normal people was like at the turn of the century and the years leading up to the revolution.' He ate a biscuit and gulped down his coffee.

'In 1910, in neighbouring Temascaltepec, 18 leagues south east of Valle, there was a large hacienda owned by a wealthy gachupine called *Jeronimo Ribera*. Ribera was a cold heartless man who drove his workers hard and paid them meagre wages. He was short and stumpy with a red face and a pinched mouth. His head was bald and shiny and he always wore a white leather glove on his left hand and carried a silver topped cane. When he was a child a rattlesnake bit him on the hand. Necrosis set in and the veterinary surgeon employed by his father had to amputate two of his fingers.

Two young brothers, called *Ricardo* and *Enrique Campos,* worked on the estate threshing corn and driving mule trains. Their widowed mother lived in a tiny house with their three little sisters in the nearby village of *Real de Arriba*. Their oldest sister had died of cholera two years before. The Campos' house was on Ribera's estate and the family were constantly in debt. Every month the bailiffs would arrive to collect the rent and threaten their mother with eviction.

After work one sunny evening in April, Ricardo and Enrique made their way to the orange orchards behind the large hacienda. The orchards were strictly out of bounds to everyone except the women who worked there picking the fruit and pruning the trees. But the brothers were thirsty after a hot day's work in the fields and Ribera had so many oranges, surely no one would notice if they ate one or two?

As they crawled under the fence into the orange groves, they could hear Ribera's bloodhounds baying in the distance. It was a glorious evening and the boys were looking forward to Saturday and the beginning of the *Semana Santa* festivities. Ricardo, aged 17 was in love with *Esperanza*, a local girl who also worked on Ribera's estate as a laundry maid, and he had been telling his friends that he planned to propose to her at the fiesta.

In the pink and orange light of dusk, the two brothers felt safe. Trees obscured the view of the house making it almost impossible for them to be seen. They would hear if anyone approached and could make their escape via an overgrown culvert which eventually led to the road and to Real de Arriba. If they were caught the worst that could happen would be that their wages could be docked for a few days.

They had picked about five oranges, when they heard the hounds again. Crouching behind some trees, they looked to see if they had been tracked. They lay in silence, and then the baying seemed to recede again. Gathering up the oranges, they headed for the fence and open cornfields. This was the only point from which they could be seen from the house. As they climbed over the fence, Enrique, the younger of the two brothers aged 15, fell and twisted his ankle. Ricardo lifted him to his feet and they limped slowly away. But they had been spotted. They could hear the hounds again and the estate manager shouting. Then they heard Ribera's voice.

'I'll teach those campesinos a lesson,' he bellowed. 'Whoever they are, I'll give them a hiding that they will never forget.'

The two young men tried running but Enrique's ankle gave way and he could only manage a limp. By now Ribera and his *mayordomo* had mounted their horses and accompanied by the dogs they had given chase. Ricardo helped his younger brother into the ditch and told him to get away as fast as he could. Once he reached the road, he would be safe. Limping down the narrow, overgrown channel, Enrique thought that his brother was not far behind. And then he slipped and fell. He slid down the muddy bank and through some brambles and onto the road. There he hid in the undergrowth for his brother. He was wet and covered in mud. The only sound that he could hear was the pounding of his heart.

Ricardo never made it into the ditch. The hounds were upon him and he was pulled to the ground and bitten in the leg and the side of the face. When Ribera dismounted he was in a rage. Clutching his cane, he thrashed the young man, raining down blows to his head and upper body. Ricardo desperately tried to protect his head with his hands, but the frenzied clubbing continued. Raul, the estate manager appealed to his master to stop:

'You will kill the boy! Hasn't he learned his lesson by now?'

But Ribera wouldn't listen. Ricardo writhed under each blow and then was ominously still; his bruised and battered hands still clutching his bloodied head. But it was too late for mercy. Ricardo's skull had been cracked and he died of a brain haemorrhage.

When Ribera realised that he had killed the young man, he felt a cold sweat running down his back. A long minute of silence passed. Raul shut his eyes and bowed his head. All that could be heard were the thirsty dogs panting and the two horses stomping in the grassy meadow.

Slowly Ribera turned to Raul, a look of cold steel in his watery blue eyes.

'It's your job to get rid of the body. Remember there were two of them and the other *cabron* got away. Mark my words, if any of this gets out, I'll drag you down to hell with me. If anyone asks; those boys were never here!' Ribera mounted his horse and trotted slowly back through the fields to the ranch house.

Enrique waited in the thick undergrowth, but his brother did not appear. By now it was dark. Enrique's ankle was swollen and he could barely stand. He wanted to return up the slippery culvert to find out what had happened to his brother but he could not climb the muddy bank. There were other routes his brother could have taken. He was probably at home, Enrique concluded.

Raul was not a bad man. Like many who worked for Ribera, he lived a hard life with a wife and three children to feed. Kneeling next to the young man's body he buried his head in his hands and wept. He did not know the Campos family well, but he knew that the boys were hardworking. He knew he had been a coward. But Ribera was a powerful man. If he had stood up to his boss there could be no doubting the outcome. Raul had played a part in the incident. He had spotted the boys and could have turned a blind eye. Who would have missed a few oranges? He had pursued the boys on horseback and with dogs and he had watched as Ribera had clubbed the young man to death. Raul knew that if he turned against his boss, he would be blamed for the murder. Who would believe the word of an uneducated *vaquero*? The punishment would be hanging! What then would happen to his family? Much as his conscience insisted that he tell the truth, he had too much to lose. He knew now that his soul was dammed. How could he attend mass and look Father *Augustin* in the face? There could be no forgiveness for his sin. With a heavy heart he lifted the boy's limp body over the saddle and leading the horse by the reins he returned to the stables. He prayed for the Campos family, but he was too ashamed to pray for his own soul.

Raul hid the body where he knew it would be discovered by all the other workers on the estate: under a huge pile of corn in the mill. When it was discovered, no one would think to point a finger at him. During Semana Santa, it was a tradition for landowners to share a small percentage of their profit with their labourers. This act was seen by the church as furthering the virtue of charity and it prevented dissent among the campesinos. Ribera was not a generous man and he resented the custom but he agreed to put aside a small stock of corn, the worst of his crop, for his labourers. On Good Friday the men and women who worked on the estate would gather to receive their sack of meal. Ricardo's body would be discovered.

No one on the estate liked Jeronimo Ribera. He was vicious and mean and cared nothing for their welfare. He was in every mind, capable of murder. When the body of their fellow worker was found, a boy whose family they all knew, they would judge for themselves who had killed him. Even if the case never came before a local magistrate, his relatives would take the law into their own hands.

On Maundy Thursday, Raul and his family closed and locked the door of their small house in Temascaltepec. They left everything behind them except a few possessions which they packed onto two mules. Their destination was the neighbouring state of Michoacan, where Raul's brother worked as a forester. They could settle there until it was safe to return. Before them were three hard days of walking through rugged mountains and forests.

Nothing but a few rumours were ever heard of Raul again in Temascaltepec. Some said he had become a blacksmith near the city of Morelia and that he spent his Sundays in church. Others claimed he had lost his entire family in an outbreak of smallpox and that he had become a bitter and broken man.

Jeronimo Ribera died mysteriously in 1918 at the age of 64. He was found hanging from a tree on the road to the spa town of Ixtapan de la Sal. The horse he had been riding, a beautiful *Andalucian* grey, was never recovered.

Enrique Campos enlisted in a local revolutionary militia in 1913, but returned five years later having been injured fighting government forces in the mountains of Guerrero. He married Esperanza's sister, Concepcion in 1921 but left Temascaltepec with his family to live in the state capital, Toluca.'

Pablo paused and ate another biscuit.

'How is it you know the details of this story so well?' I asked him. 'You recount it as if it you were there.'

Pablo looked out of the window for a moment and then he turned to me. There were tears in his eyes.

'Enrique Campos was my father. He changed his name to Ramos in 1925 to start a new life and he and his family moved to Valle where they had relatives in 1930.'

༄

CHAPTER 21

LA COCINA MEXICANA

I wonder why we can't have a horse. The Finnys, Freitags and Wiggs all have horses. We could stable it in the boiler room downstairs and it could graze on the grass in the garden and we could take it down to Valle at weekends.
But dad says it's not practical.

***

One of the many pleasures of living in Mexico was undoubtedly its food. When most people think of Mexican cuisine, tacos and enchiladas and searing hot chilli sauces usually come to mind. Few, however, have been exposed to the delicious *moles* with their ground pumpkin seeds and spicy sauces or the lime marinated seafood *ceviches*. Nor are they aware that much of our chocolate confectionery has its roots in Mexico's ancient civilisations. When the Spaniards arrived at Moctezuma's palace they found his courtiers drinking a strange beverage made from corn flour flavoured with cocoa known as atole. Today of course we call it hot chocolate!

Mexican cooking reflects the juxtaposition between ancient and modern, west and east. It's the fusion of flavours and foods brought by conquerors from Europe and mixed and enriched by native recipes and ingredients to create something unique. The first European expeditions to the America's came in search of gold but ironically it was the discovery of new and exotic foods, and ingredients, varieties of plants and domesticated wildlife that was to have the biggest historical impact on the rest of the world. Turkeys, potatoes, squashes, tomatoes, chocolate, peanuts, pineapples, melons, chillies, sugar cane and vanilla – many of the foods in fact that grace our dining tables today, were just a few of the riches that were introduced to Europe and other colonies further east by the Spaniards.

***

La *botana* is a Mexican word equivalent to *el pasa palo* from Venezuela, or the Spanish *tapa*.

Before eating a meal in Mexico it is customary to enjoy botanas and *antojitos* to whet the appetite.

A botana is the ideal companion for a beer or a midday drink and the spicier and saltier it is the better! They are usually made from fruits or vegetables such as cucumber, celery, carrots, *jicama*, orange, pineapple and prickly pear and prepared with lime, salt and chilli.

Antojitos are foods of the street, the foods of the marketplace and a centuries' old tradition. They are predominantly based on maíze flour and are often deep fried. In town squares all over Mexico you will find *chilaquiles, sopes, mojetes* and *flautas* being prepared over charcoal stoves at all times of the day as people grab a snack before going to work or returning home.

Where antojitos are eaten, close by are giant jars of *aguas frescas* - cooling beverages of blended fruit pulp. Vivid green from tart limes, pink and orange from sweet melons, they sit in colourful rows ready to quench the heat of a plate of tacos and salsa. There are nearly as many *aguas frescas* as there are fruits and they are usually made by pureeing or mashing a single fruit in ice cold water and sugar. Pineapple, melon, and citrus *aguas* are the most common, but truly exotic offerings such as *mamey*, *guanabana* and guava can also be had. Also popular is agua de *tamarindo,* a sugar-sweetened beverage made from dried tamarind pods which have been peeled, boiled in water, soaked, mashed, and strained. A passable version is easy to make, but getting it right or just getting the peel off the pods is an art in itself. Another favourite is Jamaica made from boiling hibiscus petals mixed with sugar or honey and then cooled. It is rich in antioxidants and is often prescribed by doctors for treating hepatitis.

The Mexican paleta is also unique. These are ice lollies made from fresh fruit and come in almost every flavour imaginable: lemon, orange, pineapple, tangerine, grape, coconut, ask for it and almost any paleteria in Mexico will have it. In addition to citrus fruits there are the more tropical paletas made from chunks of guava, prickly pear and papaya or combined fruits such as lime and alfalfa or passion fruit and orange. A Häagen Daz ice cream parlour opened in Valle but there was little interest in it and a few months later it closed. Even the best Italian ice cream cannot compare with the cooling freshness of a paleta on a hot, humid day in Mexico.

Horchata was originally an Iberian beverage, dating to the period of Muslim dominance in Spain and is traditionally made from tiger nuts. The Latin American version, common in Mexico, is made with rice, almonds, sugar, and cinnamon and is deliciously smooth and refreshing.

The natives, of what we now call Central America, were making alcoholic beverages from agave hearts, cactus fruits, corn, and other available ingredients since pre-Colombian times. These became integral to ceremony and ritual for indigenous people as far north as the Rockies. It is said that the inability to obtain *tiswin,* a corn-and-cactus beer the Apaches adopted from the Mexican indigenas, was one of the reasons Geronimo and his band left their reservation. In Mexico these fermented beverages made from the yucca-like *sotol* plant and agaves are known as *pulques* and remain popular drinks today.

According to the standard histories, the *conquistadores*, short on brandy, took to distilling *pulque*. Thus was born *mezcal,* a generic term for distilled liquors produced from agaves and related plants. Some of the finest of these mezcals are made from the blue agave and come from an area, mainly in the state of *Jalisco*, centred around the town of *Tequila*. Just as Champagne can only come from the Champagne region of France, Tequila can only come from a legally defined region near Tequila.

Tequila gained a reputation among mezcals similar to that of Cognac and Armagnac among brandies, then lost it in the 1950's due to the popularization of foul-tasting mixed brands brought across the border in tanker trucks from the United States. The best Tequilas are still considered crude compared to fine whiskies or brandies and should really be drunk cold but nowadays they are all too often ruined by the addition of salt and lime.

Bacanora is yet another mezcal, from a region in eastern *Sonora* surrounding the town of Bacanora. Only legal since 1992, it was distilled for generations by moonshiners and is still considered an artisanal produce. There are very few commercial brands available, but a traveller to *Hermosillo Nogales*, or any of the larger towns in Sonora should have no trouble finding either commercial bottling or quasi-bootleg Bacanora for sale. Its taste is similar to Tequila; it's made from the Pacific agave, a close relative of the Blue Agave, but with an inescapable smokiness. To call Bacanora 'barbecued Tequila' wouldn't be entirely accurate but it certainly has that hint. *Vinateros* (Bacanora producers) still roast agave hearts in ovens containing charcoal, a process abandoned long ago in Tequila and elsewhere.

Corona and *Sol* are the best known beers in Mexico and are often drunk with a slice of lime inserted into the top of the bottle. These beers are mild by European standards but still very palatable. The michelada, a sort of beer cocktail made with chilli, lime and salt is certainly an acquired taste but on a hot day and drunk with botanas and antojitos is the perfect aperitif.

***

For centuries botanas and antojitos were the main attractions of the cantinas and bars. *Manuel Payno*, in his novela '*Los Bandidos de Rio Frio*' (The bandits of Cold River), talks about the spicy *gorditas* and *quesadillas* that were available to customers in the *pulquerias*. Today these pulquerias have largely disappeared in Mexico but street stalls still serve these traditional snacks. Even in the 1960's neighbourhood cantinas competed against each other with their botanas to attract customers, and they didn't skimp on costs. Some cantinas during happy hour served up to 18 different dishes such as shrimp soup, steak tartare, and quesadillas, fried *mojarritas* with *salsa verde*, smoked pork chops, and *mariscos*. There were *cantineros* that served pork leg with prunes, *bacalao a la vizcaina*, goat, pozole or fish fillets.

***

A Mexican meal would not be complete without a *sopa*; and the king of all sopas is the Tortilla soup, also known as *Azteca* soup. Combining as it does the traditional flavours of chilli, *epazote* tomato and tortilla, in many ways it epitomises Mexican cuisine. Tortilla soup is a meal in itself with the addition of shredded chicken, cheese, avocado and cream. I invariably started my late afternoon lunch with a sopa and would list among my favourites mushroom soup, sea-food soup and the earthy coriander soup infused with wormwood and garlic.

I used to be a great apologist for the full English breakfast until I returned to Mexico and became re-acquainted with *huevos rancheros* and *huevos a la Mexicana* which became staples for me in Valle. Huevos rancheros consisted of two fried eggs, laid on a bed of tortillas and covered in a rich tomato, onion and chilli sauce. I usually ate them with bacon and refried beans which set me up for the day until the late afternoon. Huevos a la Mexicana is a variation on scrambled eggs with the addition of fried onion, tomato and of course – the ubiquitous chilli!

I believe you either love or loathe Mexican food. If like me, you become an aficionado of its infinite variety, it comes to symbolise the country itself; a fusion of cultures that make up modern Mexico.

༄

CHAPTER 22
CURAS

We are returning from Valle and have just passed through Toluca. There's a deafening explosion and Pancho starts barking and jumps into my seat. The car is spinning and when we come to a stop we are facing oncoming traffic. A lorry swerves and narrowly misses us, horn blaring. A tyre has burst, but no one is hurt. Later, dad takes us to the *Loma Linda*. We have steak with *chimichurri* sauce and chips.

***

Robert Blackmore knew Valle like no other foreigner and used his stock of well thumbed maps to explore the surrounding mountains on horseback and on foot. He was no ordinary priest. Before retiring and deciding to be ordained into the Episcopalian Church, he had run a successful family business in Mexico City. On Sundays he converted his sitting room into the 20th century version of a first century church. He and Nancy would push back their sofa and transform their dining room table into an altar and 'two or three' would gather together to share the sacraments of bread and wine.

Until 1992, when the laws regarding religious freedom were relaxed, Robert's services were illegal. In post revolutionary Mexico, a blind eye was turned towards the activities of the Roman Catholic Church banned in the 1930's when the government persecuted the clergy and closed the churches but as late as the 1970's all 'foreign' clergy were still viewed with suspicion as gringo agents from the north.

For many years Robert was the only foreigner to be invited on the annual *cabalgata*, a 30 mile riding expedition through rugged country from Valle to *Zacazonapan*, a local farming centre. The cabalgata was an all male affair, organised by ranchers, muleteers and experienced riders. It involved two long days in the saddle riding up and down steep canyons. At the cabalgata's notorious camp dinner at the end of the first day, vast quantities of alcohol and spicy food were consumed. Many riders, still hung over on the morning of the second day, never made it back into the saddle.

When questioned about his participation on these expeditions, Robert always insisted that his presence as a man of the cloth was strictly pastoral, but I could tell by the way he winked and the twinkle in his blue eyes that he too had experienced the cabalgata's full initiation.

Robert had memories of Valle stretching back five decades. Once a valley fought over by rival Otomi and Mazahua tribes, a place of worship and of war, it was transformed by the Spaniards into a prosperous town renowned throughout the State of Mexico for its rebozos and its textile industry. But the revolution ended Valle's prosperity and the town was abandoned until 1937 when government engineers began exploring the possibility of flooding part of the area for a hydroelectric plant. The project in fact offered the town a new lease of life and by 1950, Valle was once again on the map. Due to its outstanding natural beauty and its proximity to the capital, it soon became popular with riders and walkers, many of whom built small cabins in the woods as weekend retreats. The 1980's launched Valle to resort status.

The discovery of oil in the Gulf of Mexico and the rapid expansion of Mexico City's rich elite combined to turn Valle into a playground for the leisured classes. Even an ex-president bought a home in the area! The price of real estate soared and new sports clubs, restaurants and shops opened to cater for the weekenders. The excesses of the 80's ended in 1990 with two severe economic crises and life in Valle became altogether calmer. Owners of second homes like the Blackmores, continued to visit at weekends but during the week the only traffic on the streets were the blue taxis and by eight o'clock in the evening the shops were closed and Valle was silent with only a few stray dogs roaming the streets.

***

Padre Ruffo was the local Catholic priest. He was a small, cheerful looking man with a shiny, bald head and spectacles. He believed in miracles and many were the stories he told of visions, supernatural healings and wonders. His favourite story was how *El Cristo Negro* hanging above the altar in the church of Santa Maria, received its name.

In the days of *Porfirio Diaz*, there were two rival groups of indigenas, one a Mazahua family, the other Otomi. The Mazahua worked as farm labourers on the estate of a rich Spanish landowner in the village of San Gaspar.

The Spaniard commissioned the building of a private chapel on his grounds, and brought a huge, oak crucifix from Spain which soon gained fame in the area as a source of miracles. Each day, a steady stream of indigenas would visit the chapel to pray at the foot of the cross. Some came for healing, others to worship and each week a new miracle was performed.

The landowner soon tired of the endless queues of pilgrims that gathered daily for a glimpse of the Christ and was going to ban his workers from frequenting his chapel, but it had become so popular and its fame so widespread that he was persuaded by the Bishop of Toluca to build a hermitage on his grounds dedicated to the crucifix.

Then, during Semana Santa one year during the Easter celebrations, Otomi and Mazahua rivals clashed in a drunken brawl and in the ensuing riot, the chapel was burnt down. The following day when the fire had been extinguished the Mazahua searched among the ruins of the hermitage for the crucifix and miraculously, they found it intact but it was as black as ebony. The discovery of the undamaged Christ was taken as a divine message that there should be peace among the indigenas and it was decided that the newly resurrected crucifix should be transferred to the larger, grander church of Santa Maria at the southern end of Valle.

A few years later, an earthquake hit the town destroying the nave where the black Christ had hung. Several weeks after the destruction of the church when rebuilding had begun, the black Christ mysteriously re-appeared above the altar and it continues to be a source of miracles and the destination for pilgrims from all over the state of Mexico.

CHAPTER 23

LA POSADA

Jason and Lucinda are flying back to England today. Fiona and I are crying. We won't see them for three months. Jason and Lucinda are dressed in their uniforms. Even Lucinda is wearing a tie. The airport is huge and there are hundreds of people milling about. An American man with long hair and a red bandana tied around his head is kissing a pretty woman with blonde hair, on the lips. They are still kissing and mum tells me it's rude to stare. We say goodbye to Jason and Lucinda. They disappear behind a barrier waving. Mum says for a treat she will take us to *Vips* for a hamburger and fries.

***

The arrival of December heralded the beginning of the *posada* season. I loved December in Valle; it brought back many happy memories of childhood Christmases spent in the village back in the

1970's when we used to rent a house in Avandaro. Then, several events made the season particularly special. There was the annual paper chase, a home grown version of a drag hunt with riders on horses playing the foxes, leaving trails of confetti for the hunt to follow. The paper chase was a great reunion when friends would meet for a day out on horseback in the hills. There must have been close on 80 riders taking part in the paper chase each year aged from between five and 60 and that didn't include the many Vallesanos who also joined us. We would meet at the *glorietta* in Avandaro at about ten o'clock in the morning. There were usually four or five 'foxes' of all ages, selected primarily on the their riding ability. The 'foxes' wore red bandanas and were given half an hour's head start and bags of confetti. The aim of the game was to catch the foxes by following the trails, some of which were false and led nowhere. To catch a 'fox' a rider had to literally tag him or her, so speed, agility and the ability to handle your steed were essential.

Usually the paper chase lasted several hours ending in the early afternoon at the Finny's ranch at *Barranca Fresca* with a huge barbecue. I had vivid memories of these chases; they were the highlight of my year. I recall being bitterly disappointed when I was given *Panzon*, a fat little pony that refused to canter and I was therefore left behind to ride with the toddlers and their minder. I remember another year the exhilaration of riding *Mustang*, probably the fastest gelding in Valle. He was a beautiful light brown horse with a golden mane and could canter and gallop for hours it seemed. I have a memory too of being hugely envious when my closest friend Jaime Finny (then only aged 10 and two years older than me) was chosen to be a fox. That was the biggest accolade that an adult could bestow on a young rider. It meant you had passed a rite of passage; you had been initiated into the highest equestrian order!

Barranca Fresca was a mountain paradise. John Finny had discovered the idyllic spot on a ride early in the 70's and vowed that one day he would own the land and build his dream ranch there. It was situated by the side of Cerro Gordo, high above Valle in a beautiful valley flanked by rivers, woods and upland meadows spotted with wild flowers. Years before it had been a pig farm and the ruins of an old house and the sties now covered in moss and vines could still be found in the tangled undergrowth. My father was with John

Finny when they came across this 'Shangri-La'. They had been riding through the hills for several hours when they took a path that meandered up the side of Cerro Gordo and then weaved left. And then there was an unexpected opening in the woods and they rode out into open meadows and were greeted by thousands of butterflies fluttering in the late morning sun.

It was years before John was able to buy the land, but it became the traditional venue for the paper chase barbecue and a collective symbol of everyone's dreams and aspirations.

It was at the end of one memorable paper chase that I burnt myself badly. I was playing football with Jaime and Peter Davey on uneven ground when I tripped and fell headlong into the glowing embers of a fire. One hand broke my fall; the other fell into the hot ash. I remember my arm being wrapped in a poultice of honey and herbs by a *curandero* and feeling the intense heat draining away like liquid as the old *cacique* muttered something incoherent.

When John and Susan Finny built their ranch, they created something very special. There was a modest, comfortable log house, stables and the most beautiful English garden. There were corrals for horses, fish ponds and a tennis court. Getting to Barranca Fresca was still a small adventure. There was no paved road, just forest tracks that became muddy trenches in the rainy season leaving the ranch in splendid isolation, remotely situated in lush hills.

***

Posadas formed part of the Advent celebrations leading up to Christmas Eve. In every neighbourhood they re-enacted the journey taken by Mary and Joseph to Bethlehem for the census and their search for accommodation on the night that Jesus was born.

Fundraising for the posadas began in November with door to door collections and appeals during mass for contributions. Choosing the boys and girls to represent the various characters in the Biblical story started in October with auditions in local schools. Young girls aged about 12 usually played Mary whilst Joseph was often a few years older. And then there was the cast of shepherds, wise men, angels, inn keepers, high priests and kings. Each barrio in Valle held its own posada. The start of the posada was a local church or chapel where neighbours would congregate holding candles and lanterns at dusk. A local family would volunteer to act as the innkeeper where the young couple eventually found lodgings. They would help organise the event and provide food and drink for everyone at the end of the procession.

My barrio, Santa Maria, held its posada on December the 18th. There must have been 300 people gathered outside the church expectantly. A cool breeze flickered through the candlelight and the street was full of merry, smiling faces. I spotted *Doña Maria*, the overweight greengrocer who used to complain to me that her husband beat her. *Chiro*, the local vet was there too. We had met the week before during a half marathon. When the church bells tolled seven o'clock the procession began. Mary and Joseph led the way. They looked shy and self conscious surrounded by their friends and family. Mary wore a cream coloured dress and a white veil and rode side saddle on an old donkey led by Joseph. He wore a beige, knee length tunic and sandals and carried a staff. Behind them, the parish banner was mounted on a cart drawn by two mules. The shepherds and wise men followed and behind them the rest of the parish, candles in hand. Posada carols were sung. Everyone knew the words off by heart (except for me) though most were singing out of tune. The result was a curious chant.

Four times along the route, Mary and Joseph sought accommodation only to be turned away. But an hour later, at the end of Calle San Sebastian, *Carmela Lopez* was waiting outside her house with its wooden balcony and pots of poinsettias. She welcomed us with tamales and atole and hot sweet *ponche*. People brought crispy tacos with shredded chicken and lettuce and green tomato sauce, corn on the cob with cream and chilli powder and quesadillas to share. A piñata was strung up across the street filled with fruit and sticky sweets and children took turns to hit the clay effigy with a broomstick until it broke showering the ground with confectionery. San Sebastian gradually filled with people joining in from other fiestas. Someone brought out a large pan and deep fried *chicharon* and a cool box with natural fruit ice lollies appeared. A mariachi band arrived and soon there was dancing and the whole street seemed to sway. By any standards, this had been a good posada.

***

When I was a child growing up in Mexico the best posada was hosted by *Feliciano Bejar*. He was a friend of my parents and a world renowned artist. Born in 1920, Feliciano was self taught and one of the most influential sculptors and philanthropists of his generation. Bejar regenerated his local community building a small village for the poorest people in his neighbourhood. It was aesthetically a work of art. All the buildings were constructed using traditional materials: the houses were made from white washed adobe with terracotta roof tiles and reclaimed wood and the streets were cobbled. Every dwelling was supplied with sanitation, gas and electricity and there were co-operative shops, a medical centre, orphanage and other facilities. Every Christmas, Bejar held a traditional posada to which he invited friends and family to celebrate with the people from the community. There was a magical feeling about the place. The streets were decked with papel picado, Christmas lights, lanterns, sparklers and piñatas and there were stalls serving tamales and punch. Fireworks lit up the dark night sky and the air smelt of cordite and spit roasted chickens.

***

My brother Jason and his wife Jean arrived on the 20th of December to spend Christmas with me. He had been on business in Denver, Colorado and being in North America was too big an opportunity to miss not coming down to Mexico. He, like me had not been back for 17 years and was excited by the prospect of that metaphorical crossing of the Alamo from north to south.

Jason was 15 when we left Mexico and had clear, vivid memories of our time there. He and Jean flew to Benito Juarez airport and then hired a car and drove down to Valle. I was amazed at his confidence and ability in finding his way through Mexico City and down to Valle in the dark after so many years. The city had changed almost beyond recognition in the interim decades.

'I just got onto the *Periferico* and followed signs for Toluca,' he said nonchalantly. 'Apart from the heavy traffic, there was nothing to it!'

We had arranged to meet in the zocalo at eight o'clock. It had been almost three months since I had seen my brother and the combination of seeing me and returning to Valle was an emotional moment for him. There were tears in his eyes when he hugged me.

'It's just as I remembered it,' he said looking around, 'though a bit cleaner and I don't recall so many taxis – but it's the same; that smell of the hills and the tacos and wood smoke is the same!'

Jason and Jean stayed with me for two weeks. We took a trip to *Malinalco* to see the Aztec temple there and spent a night in *Ixtapan de la Sal*. Malinalco has always been associated with magic and sorcery due to the legend that it was the home of the goddess of the underworld, *Malinalxóchil*.

The Aztecs conquered the area in the 1470's, and established a sanctuary for their military elite, the warriors of the Eagle and Jaguar. The complex was built on the *Cerro de los Idolos* (Hill of the Idols), over an older ceremonial site. The main attraction is the *Cuauhcalli* or House of Eagles which was hewn out of mountainside.

***

Nancy and Robert shared their city residence with Lorna, their second eldest daughter, and they invited us to join their family for lunch on Christmas Day. We drove up to the city on Christmas Eve and spent the evening driving around the centre looking at the Christmas lights. Mexico's festive lights are like no others. They are huge and elaborate and depict various stages of the Christmas story from the voyage to Bethlehem to the birth of Christ. When we were children my father used to take us out on one of the nights leading up to Christmas just to see the lights, ending up somewhere like the recently opened Pizza Hut for a meal.

I was amazed at how well Jason remembered the streets of the DF. He wasn't fazed by the onslaught of traffic, the blaring horns of the *peseros* the perilous manoeuvres of other drivers, the street vendors crowding in on the car at every traffic light or the window cleaners who almost threw themselves onto the bonnet to get a swipe at the windscreen before demanding payment.

We drove down tree lined *Reforma* and *Insurgentes* and ended up at *Sanborns*, that timeless shop and cafe where the waitresses wear winged paper blouses and long skirts and you can buy Cuban cigars, Scotch Whisky and shortbread. The retail company was founded in Mexico City in 1903 by Californian immigrants Walter and Frank Sanborn. The original location and its lunch counter, across from the main Mexico City post office, is still in operation.

During the Mexican Revolution, Emiliano Zapata's revolutionaries used a branch of Sanborns as a rendezvous. Sepia photos show *Zapatistas* enjoying their first restaurant meal in Sanborns' dining room. In 1919, Sanborns acquired its most famous branch, the 16th century House of Tiles (*La Casa de los Azulejos*) a major Mexico City tourist attraction and now a national monument. This is probably the world's only department store decorated with a mural by *José Clemente Orozco*.

We spent Christmas Day at Carlos and Rosemary Gottfried's house in *Coyoacan,* once a leafy suburb of the city and home to *Frida Kahlo, Diego Rivera and Leon Trotsky. Rosemary* was the Blackmore's eldest daughter and she and her family lived in an enormous house down a cobbled street just off Coyoacan's central square. There must have been 30 of us sitting down to Christmas lunch in the spacious conservatory. There was Nancy and Robert, their son Gerald and their three daughters; Rosemary, Lorna and Vivienne. There were grandchildren, husbands and wives, Mario and Martha Gottfried (Carlos' parents), former maids and employees and even former partners! We drank Champagne and there were speeches and a traditional roast turkey, pudding and cake and for a moment, pulling the crackers and reading the cheap jokes, I almost forgot that we were still in Mexico. As we were leaving late in the evening, Martha Gottfried invited me to their house in Valle.

'When Jason and Jean have returned to England you must have dinner with us. I hate to think of you all alone,' she said handing me my coat. 'We'll invite some pretty young things and see if we can hook you up with someone,' she said smiling.

***

Three days later a friend from London arrived and was waiting patiently on my doorstep when we returned from *La casa de Artesanias*. 'I presume you received my letter?' said Hilary, a wide grin on her face. I introduced her to Jason and Jean and we went into the house and Jean made a pot of tea.

I had received Hilary's missive but knowing that letters could take weeks to wend their way to England, I had no way of communicating our plans to visit Mexico City for Christmas. Hilary had done well in finding her way down to Valle without precise instructions, but then she was a very experienced investigative journalist!

We had met the previous year through a mutual friend. She was originally from New Zealand but her Antipodean accent was very mild and she had no intention of returning home. Hilary had long blonde hair, clear blue eyes and a tanned complexion. She was in her early thirties.

I was hugely envious of Hilary. She had just secured a much coveted interview with Ranulph Fiennes who had recently returned from his latest crossing of Antarctica with Mike Stroud. I had been trying to interview him for months but every time I contacted his agent, he was either on the lecture circuit or on an expedition.

Hilary stayed a couple of nights and then headed south to Chiapas and Guatemala. Just after New Year, Jason and Jean returned to England. On New Year's Eve, I took them to the Monarca for a comida corrida. We began talking about New Year's resolutions when Jean said, 'Instead, lets make some predictions,' and she thought for a moment. 'My prediction for you Marcus, is that you will fall in love out here; so what do you think to that?

***

Martha and Mario Gottfried owned a large weekend house with a swimming pool in the barrio of Santa Maria. I had not been there for over 20 years but when I opened the gate and walked past the pool towards the front door, memories of New Year's Eve parties back in the 70's came flooding back. I remembered aged six getting very drunk when Maria Freitag plied me with a glass of rum and coke. I recalled too, a treasure hunt at night through the cemetery and being told by Jaime Finny that the ghost of *El Viejo* (a wizened old man) – haunted the marshy land by the lakeside and made his home in the graveyard.

Unfortunately there were no 'pretty young things' sitting down to dinner that Saturday night at the Gottfrieds. I was conspicously the youngest guest there by about 40 years. Martha seated me next to an elderly lady from Alabama with white hair and bifocals. Half way through the meal she turned to me as if continuing some previous conversation that we had had and said, 'Niggers ain't what they used to be. Ma folks had a nigger boy by the name of Sylvester when we was livin' in Sweet Creek. Now for a nigger, he was a fine man; respectful and the like, but nowadays all you hear is them rapin' and killin'.' And she smiled inanely at me through watery brown eyes.

CHAPTER 24

UNA CARTA

We arrive in San *Cristobal de las Casas* in the dead of night. The town's cobbled streets are silent and deserted. We are looking for the hotel. We are told it's on a hillside overlooking the valley. We drive out of town and see a dim light at the entrance to the cemetery. Dad needs to ask for directions again. An old man, blind with white cataracts leans out of the small cabin.

That night I have nightmares.

***

The New Year brought a letter from Hilary.

'Dear Marcus

I am writing to you from San Cristobal de las Casas,' the letter began.

'Just a few hours ago the zocalo here was full of carousing tourists bringing in the New Year and singing in half a dozen languages. By one o'clock in the morning there were only a few diehards left, myself among them in a night gradually growing damp and misty. At around two o'clock the troops of *El Ejercito Zapatista de la Liberacion Nacional* gunned down the doors of the town hall, chased the guards away and took over the city.

At dawn, the rebels began throwing documents out of the town hall window, dragging furniture, filing cabinets and ageing computers out into the town square where they threw them into a tangled pile. I had planned to spend the day in nearby indian villages so I had woken up and left my hotel room at about five o'clock. On the corner of the square, standing behind a barricade, was a small man with a red bandana mask and green uniform holding an ancient shotgun. I gestured to him asking if it was okay to go past and he nodded handing me a notice. It read *'Declaracion de Guerra. Hoy decimos basta.'* – (declaration of war, today we say that we have had enough). Even with my meagre Spanish, I knew what it meant!

The document spelt out the desperation of 500 years of pain and injustice meted out to the indigenous people of the *Lacondon* region. They had nothing it said; no land, no work, no health care, no education and no freedom. Their forests had been destroyed and over 5,000 indigenas gaoled without charge. They were persecuted and impoverished. Now they had had enough. If no one listened to their grievances they were prepared to die fighting to regain their lives and dignity.

Milling around the square were about 250 rebel soldiers dressed in newly sewn green uniforms with red kerchiefs around their necks. They carried a motley collection of weapons: a couple of AK47 assault rifles, but mostly single bore shotguns, hunting knives, machetes and crude bayonets on sticks. They were small, fine boned men and women, some no more than teenagers. Four girls with long, black plaited hair wearing baseball caps emblazoned with the words 'Top Gun' and 'Guns and Roses' stood nervously guarding the entrance to the town's municipal buildings. The square was carpeted in papers, files and documents, which the townspeople were rifling through. Others were eagerly distributing the '*de-*

claracion.' As nine o'clock approached the zocalo filled with people. Groups sat under the colonnades in deep discussion. In one corner of the square some rebels were piling what looked like the entire contents of the chemists'; everything from medicines and crutches to toothbrushes, condoms and sanitary towels. One of them told me that they were gathering medical supplies in preparation for the arrival of the Mexican army. On the walls of the town hall, scrawled graffiti proclaimed *'Queremos comida, vivienda y dignidad,'* – (we want food, housing and dignity).

The constant rumour around the town was that the Mexican army was on its way from the military garrison at *Tuxtla Gutierrez*. The town's people apparently, were more fearful of the arrival of the National Guard than they were of the guerrilla force. The leaders of the rebellion were ensconced in the mayor's offices. In one room, a handful of soldiers were trying to hammer their way into the treasury's safe, egged on by a crowd.

By 10 o'clock there was still no sign of any approach by the authorities. There was no shouting, no rebel rousing, only soft modulated voices deferential to questions. It all began to feel quite surreal as we got used to the guns and the unsmiling but not aggressive faces of the rebels. Many of them were exhausted, leaning against each other or draped over their rucksacks dozing under trees. Tourists milled around taking photographs and there was almost a festive feel in the air.

At midday the rebels held a conference. Reporters and journalists from the state capital arrived. They were rude, arrogant men who belittled the indians when they were asked to produce press credentials. They crushed around diminutive *Commandante Felipe*, who wore a big straw hat and stood on a chair to speak. He spoke gently, leaning back slightly from the thrust of the microphones and tape recorders. He claimed that most people in Mexico were ignorant of the plight of his people. They knew nothing of the persecution, starvation and displacement of the indigenous tribes. This was the reason why they had revolted. He reassured the public that their grievance was with the government; that they would not harm members of the public – but they had declared war on the Federal Government.

Foreign tourists expressed amazement at how the rebel army could have organised such an effective attack with no warning and how the national government had been taken completely by surprise. There were a couple of panics. At one point someone ran into the square shouting that the army had arrived and the atmosphere changed dramatically. You could almost smell the fear in the air. People began to run in all directions in search of shelter. I ducked under some scaffolding and began to shoot film of the chaos. But within a few minutes it became clear that it had been a false alarm and people began slowly to return to the square, although the rebel soldiers now stayed close to the town hall, alert, no longer chatting and laughing.

At two in the afternoon, three small military planes circled overhead prompting some to shout that the town was about to be bombed. Some rebels pointed their guns hopefully but after a few menacing turns, the planes disappeared.

At dusk, another meeting took place. The two commanders who had spoken earlier repeated their grievances. Then another came forward. He was tall and wore a black balaclava. He introduced himself as *Commandante Marcos*. He spoke eloquently, soft toned, the tongue of an educated man. People whispered that he was rumoured to be Swiss or German – a communist agitator based in Guatemala who had inflamed the passions of the local *indigenas*. Marcos spelt out what other actions had been taken by his guerrilla force. There had been fighting in *Ocosingo* he reported, where two of his soldiers had been killed and four taken prisoner. His forces had besieged the villages of *Las Margaritas* and *Altamirano*. All the roads leading out of San Cristobal had been blocked and his forces had already attacked a column of army vehicles.

Suddenly there was a loud bang and the crowd rippled with panic. For a few long minutes we were poised to run. Then Marcos reassured us. 'Go home,' he said 'and stay home.' With nightfall it all seemed more frightening. The rebels were preparing for an imminent attack. I was with a Colombian woman who had been a stalwart all day, supporting other hysterical tourists. She told me how she remembered the army arriving one night in her village and how they took away five young men, all friends of her brothers. They were never seen again. We returned to our hotel rooms and listened for sounds of battle; but none came.

At five o'clock the following morning, the second of January, I got up, dressed and stepped nervously into the street. I had to make a call to the BBC and wanted to see if the rebel forces were still there. It was foggy and I could barely see. I then overheard two locals saying that the Zapatistas had gone; they had retreated into the forests where they stood more of a chance of outwitting the Federal Army. I rang the BBC and half an hour later was on the last bus to leave San Cristobal in a convoy bound for Tuxtla.'

And the letter ended.

***

I rushed out to Valle's only paper shop and scoured the magazine racks for foreign media. I picked up the latest edition of Time Magazine, but there was nothing on Mexico except ongoing negotiations on the NAFTA free trade agreement. I looked for evidence of the uprising in national newspapers, but there was nothing. It wasn't until 10 days later that headlines reported: 'Zapatistas massacre local people in San Cristobal' – these later proved to be totally unfounded!

CHAPTER 25

TAXIS Y TAXISTAS

There's a cocktail party in the house tonight. There are waiters and waitresses dressed in black and white standing among the guests with trays of food and drinks. The ambassador and his wife are coming in a black Rolls Royce. I am dressed in my pyjamas and dressing gown lying on the landing watching through the banisters, waiting for the ambassador to come in his black Rolls Royce.

***

After the Christmas holidays, my life took on a more regular routine, uninterrupted by the many festivals and national holidays that had punctuated the previous term. From January, the dry season established itself. The mornings remained cool and fresh but by midday the air was hot and dusty and the sun relentlessly bright. The brilliant blue skies of the rainy season had given way to pale blue heavens filled with high, puffy white clouds. The mud, which we cursed in the rainy season, that clung to boots and shoes and was brought into classrooms was now a layer of fine, brown powder whisked up by frequent breezes and whirlwinds. The earth smelt altogether different: not rich, damp and almost edible as in the rainy season but burnt and lifeless. By the middle of February the countryside looked exhausted. Dry, crisp brown maize leaves rattled in the wind, the wild flowers had shrivelled and the trees were grey with dust. Cattle, donkeys and horses looked tired and thirsty and life generally seemed to function at a slower, more lethargic pace. But I liked the dry season, neither more nor less than the rainy season, but for different reasons. Both had their individual characteristics. Both were welcomed at first as a change from monotony and later cursed for dragging on too long. The same comments were heard at the beginning and end of each season: 'I wish this would end; I am sick of the damp, the water and the mud,' people would say after three months of rain and, 'If only the rains would come, the house is so dusty and the heat seems to be making everyone so bad tempered,' they would say towards the end of the dry season.

***

By the middle of the second term, I had settled into life at La Escuela Valle de Bravo. In addition to administrative duties, I taught Year Five. There were 12 children aged between nine and 10 – four girls and eight boys. Half of them were from families who had moved to Valle from Mexico City. The children from wealthy families were all spoilt but the boys were especially so. Boys in Mexico are their family's princes. Rich Mexican boys are like emperors! *Joaquin* was particularly spoilt. He was small and blonde and an exceptional footballer. His parents owned a beautiful hotel and restaurant in town and an avocado ranch on the western end of the lake. Neither of them worked as such. The hotel and ranch were entertaining hobbies managed by local Vallesanos. Joaquin had every toy and gadget that a boy could dream of: motorbikes, jet skies, and computers, video games, expensive watches even his own full sized football pitch and tennis court. For his tenth birthday, his parents arranged for players on the Toluca football team to come and demonstrate their skills and Joaquin flew to the U.S for two weeks in their private jet for the World Cup.

Before a camping trip one weekend, I set the children some work listing the 10 most important items to take with them. The girls in the class came up with sensible ideas. They listed matches, sleeping bags, tents, food and insect repellent and other useful items. The boys were useless. One wrote, 'My maid,' at the top of his list. Another listed his remote control helicopter.

The other half of fourth grade were local children. There was Ludwig, whose father worked for the Electrical Commission. He was dark skinned with shiny black hair. *Alexis'* parents owned the bookshop in town and *Ivan's* family ran a local fish restaurant.

***

Although working at the school was by no means stressful, by two o'clock in the afternoon the children and staff were ready to go home, especially in the dry season when the heat sapped everyone's energy. When I wasn't rushing home to teach a private class, I often caught a taxi into the centre of town sharing it with up to four others, and ate a leisurely lunch at the Monarca. Taxis were the only efficient form of public transport in Valle and there were hundreds of them; 350 to be exact or such was the figure quoted whenever the subject of taxis was brought up, and this was frequent. The number of taxis on the street was generally regarded as a nuisance. They were the cause of unnecessary traffic and congestion and considered an eye sore due to their size and pale blue colour. No one doubted that taxis were useful. The local buses were few and couldn't be relied upon but it was the number of taxis and how they appeared in the first place that was often debated.

At the height of Mexico's oil boom in the mid 80's, when the price of real estate in Valle soared higher than Acapulco, cash incentives were offered to Vallesanos by property developers in exchange for selling their plots of land in and around the town. Many succumbed to the temptation of making quick and seemingly easy money and sold up. Developers promptly moved in, built luxurious second homes and sold them for enormous profits to rich city dwellers wishing to buy weekend houses.

Some Vallesanos used their money to start businesses as shopkeepers or lake tour guides. Most of them, not used to such large amounts of money, were ill advised and squandered their newly found fortunes. They quickly became destitute and resorted to squatting in corrugated iron shacks on marshy ground at the lakeside or above the town where they tapped into the water and electricity supply and polluted the streams with domestic waste and sewage. A small number of the new rich however invested in taxis. To begin with there were only a few blue taxis on the streets of Valle. They were in constant demand, ferrying people around town but also further afield making long distance trips to the coast and to Mexico City. They worked long hours, kept what they earned, formed their own association and profitted. Within a couple of years however the fleet of 20 blue taxis had more than tripled and eight years on the taxi business had got out of control. The original taxi drivers lobbied local government and demanded tighter restrictions on the granting of licences, but still more blue taxis cluttered the streets. The new taxi drivers formed their own splinter organisations and officials in the Department of Transport, who were responsible for issuing licences profitted from the new businesses.

By 1993, the taxi industry had reached saturation point. There were too many taxis and not enough customers. A few taxi drivers sold up and moved from Valle to neighbouring towns. The Department of Transport was persuaded to see the sense in tighter licensing laws and by 1994, every taxi driver was required to carry a standard list of tariffs and a registration number but the volume of taxis still in circulation around the streets of Valle remained ridiculously high.

***

Outside Mexico City's Observatorio station I flagged down a taxi and directed the driver to take me to *Serapio Rendon* where I was due for a meeting with the school's solicitor. As soon as I was seated in the back of the little green Beetle, the meter ticking away, I was the captive audience for my gregarious driver, a small rotund man with a goatee beard who sat chewing a toothpick.

Once he established that I spoke Spanish, there was no stopping him. He didn't want a conversation since he wouldn't let me get a word in edge ways. What he wanted was to talk to an anonymous silent audience, first about football, then about Americans and finally about martial arts films, which he insisted were the best films a man could watch – no question about it *'Amigo.'*

'In the 70's there was el señor Bruce Lee. Now he was a master. Pow, pow,' shouted *Luis Gutierrez* as he took his hands off the steering wheel and chopped the air with them. 'Then in the 80's there was el gringo Chuck Norris, but he was a *pendejo*. They say no one is better than the big guy Stevan Segal. I have seen his latest film seven times!' he said as he swerved to avoid a head on collision with a *pesero* bus and a motorcycle. 'But that Belgian guy – Jean Claude something or other, they say he is a *pinche* maricon!'

By the time we had reached my destination, Luis had given me a potted history of the genre accompanied by sound effects and actions that I will never forget.

***

As I sat in the station waiting for my bus back to Valle, I read the chilling account of a German tourist who had recently been abducted whilst taking a taxi form the international airport to his downtown hotel.

Axel Buellesbach arrived on an early evening Lufthansa flight from Frankfurt and planned to spend two weeks touring Mayan ruins in Chiapas and the Yucatan.

After retrieving his luggage, he went through customs and out through the sliding glass doors of the arrivals terminal. It had been a long and tiring flight and Axel was anxious to get to his hotel to sleep off his jet lag. The arrivals terminal at Benito Juarez Airport can be a bewildering and disorientating place. As you wheel your trolley out into the open concourse you are met by a sea of eager faces and a cacophony of shouting tour operators brandishing placards and gesticulating taxi drivers touting for business. Instead of heading for the official taxi rank, Axel followed the first taxi driver that presented him with credentials.

'How was I to know,' Axel was quoted to have said. 'The man wore a suit and had an identity card pinned to his jacket and insisted on carrying my luggage. Of course I thought he was genuine – I had no reason to question him.'

Axel followed the taxi driver outside where a small yellow saloon with TAXI written across the doors was parked at the curb side.

'The driver opened the rear door for me and placed my luggage in the boot. When he got into the car I gave him directions to the Hotel *Presidente* near the main square. The driver presented me with a list of tariffs and told me it would cost 50 pesos. We set off out of the airport and joined the heavy evening traffic following signs for the city centre. After about 20 minutes, we pulled up outside some shops and the driver indicated in broken English that he wanted to buy some cigarettes. I thought he was taking a bit of a liberty, but since the fare was based on a fixed rate, it didn't really bother me and I was too tired to protest. A few minutes later, the driver came out of the shop accompanied by a tall man dressed in a heavy black overcoat and a baseball cap. I presumed they were friends and thought nothing of it. But then suddenly this second man opened the car door and jumped on top of me. I was so taken aback and shocked, I didn't react immediately. Then when I struggled to get free it was too late. The man produced a syringe and hypodermic needle from his pocket and plunged it into my arm. A few seconds later, I was paralysed. Although I was still fully conscious, I couldn't feel a thing. The car set off at a screeching pace and I was blind folded, tied and gagged. There was no conversation between the two men, but about 10 minutes later the car stopped again. I heard the men get out and then the car door opened. I was dragged out of the back of the car and bundled into a huge blanket and then I must have lost consciousness.'

Axel was taken to a surgery where under general anaesthetic, his left eye was removed. Fortunately for Axel, he could recall nothing of the terrifying ordeal. What he did remember was waking up the following morning on a rubbish dump somewhere on the outskirts of the city. A large bandage had been wrapped around his head that extended over his left eye socket and was secured with gauze and surgical tape. His khaki sleeveless jacket and trousers were covered in blood and he had been robbed of his wallet and watch. He was weak, filthy and still heavily sedated. Some children rummaging in the rubbish spotted him as he stood up, weaved about among the debris and then stumbled and fell again. They were only young and laughed hysterically at the sight of this strange apparition, but when the man did not rise again they realized something was wrong and the eldest, a boy aged about nine, ran off towards the shanty town for help. About 20 minutes later he returned with a group of men. They helped Axel to his feet and poured water into his parched mouth. A few minutes later, a police car and an ambulance arrived and Axel was taken to the ABC General Hospital.

After several days in intensive care, Axel woke up to find three men in dark suits sitting at his bedside. One of them introduced himself as the German consul. The other two were both federal agents: one from the FBI and the other, his Mexican counterpart.

During extensive interviews, Axel was told that he had been the arbitrary victim of an international ring of organ exporters that illicitly provided transplant organs such as corneas to private clinics in North America and Europe.

'Is there anything else you can recall?' asked the American agent. 'The vehicle's registration number? Or any distinctive features of either the taxi driver or his associate?'

'Other than what I have told you, no,' replied Axel. 'I was tired and looking forward to a good night's sleep and my two week holiday. The last thing on my mind was the taxi's number plate or the thought that I might wake up the following morning on a rubbish heap with only one eye!'

∽

CHAPTER 26

LA CASA DE LOS ESPIRITUS

Adela has been with us since she was 16. She came to work for mum and dad in *Ecuador*. When they moved to Argentina she asked mum and dad if she could come too. She has been with us ever since. Adela says she loves Mexico. She always sits on Jose's car and chats to him when he comes to deliver eggs. She laughs and smiles. Jason says she's in love with him.

***

Patti Muller used to live at number 98, Culebra Street in the days when the house was haunted. Then in 1983, the spirits were exorcised by Padre *Domingo* and another family moved in. The house was never the same again.

***

'I moved into Culebra with my son when he was four years old. We did not have much money so we took in a lodger to help pay the bills and the rent. In those days, the house was rather decrepit and the garden required a lot of work. But it had great charm and when we moved in one hot day in the dry season, there seemed to be a good feeling about the place. This sense that somehow the house or some spirit residing in it liked us or was on our side was to be confirmed time and time again over the months that we lived there.

I began to believe that we shared the house with some benevolent spirit about two months after we moved in. I had gone shopping with *Pedrito* one wet evening in the rainy season and had returned to an empty dark house. *Roberto*, the old philosopher who lodged with us, was away in Mexico at the time so there was no one to welcome us home or to help me carry my son and all our shopping in from the car. We were dripping wet when we opened the gate to the house and I remember thinking how wonderful it would be if we could come home to a nice warm house with maybe a little gentle music playing.

Then all of a sudden, the lights in the house came on, but I did not feel alarmed by what had happened. In fact it seemed quite normal. I thought about it a few times that night as I lay in bed, but later almost forgot the incident. Perhaps it had been a freak occurrence. I knew nothing about electricity, so I put it down to the stormy weather. They say that strange things happen in the rainy season in Mexico – there is so much static in the air.

But two weeks later another mysterious thing happened which once again made me think that there was some force or spirit in the house that wished to protect us. At the time we possessed very little furniture. My bed consisted of a large mattress, which I laid on the sitting room floor. Pedrito slept on an inflatable lilo between the mattress and the wall. The upstairs bedroom was too damp to use and the roof leaked.

One night, I suddenly felt something shake my arm and I heard a gentle but urgent voice in my ear. To this day, I cannot recall whether I was awake or dreaming. Nor do I remember if the voice was that of a man or a woman. I knew that I was awake however, when I opened my eyes and saw a large black scorpion on the wall about an inch away from Pedrito's head. Luckily I had a book beside my mattress so I picked it up and squashed it. Every year, children in Mexico die from scorpion stings, often in their sleep. Someone or something was looking out for us that night.

There were many incidents, some so small that now looking back it is easy to explain them away as coincidences. But the strange thing is that these things only happened in that house. They have never occurred to me since and never before. On another occasion it was one of those times when Roberto was spending the weekend in Valle. It was early in the evening and I was cooking supper. Pedrito and Roberto were playing cards and making a lot of noise laughing and chatting in the living room. By now we had mended the roof and used the upstairs room as a study and occasional bedroom. As I was cooking I thought I heard a familiar voice. I knew that it wasn't Pedrito's or Roberto's – I could hear them playing behind me, so I turned to see if anyone else had come into the room. No one had. The voice was urgent and although I don't recall the exact words, it seemed to be telling me to go upstairs.

I dropped what I was doing and ran. As I climbed the staircase, I could hear Roberto below me saying 'Woman, what has got into you?' I did not expect to see what I did. At the end of the attic room, which stretched the length of the house, a curtain by the window was on fire. Flames were licking up towards the wooden roof beams and there was a quiet crackling sound of burning material. I screamed for help and told Pedro to get out of the house. Soon Roberto and I had put the fire out with buckets of water but we had been very lucky. If those dry beams had caught, we might never have got out of the house. Later that week an electrician confirmed that old, faulty wiring had caused the fire. We had to re-wire the whole house. Two years later I bought my little cabin in *El Deposito* and we moved out of La Culebra. The new owners were superstitious and had the house exorcised by Padre Domingo.'

⁂

CHAPTER 27
PICARUELOS

Bappy died last week, so mum has gone to England to be with Nana. Bappy had a wooden leg. He lost his real leg in the First World War. I touched it once. It felt hard. Nana says he was given a medal for defusing a bomb. Mum said she would buy me a toy tank from Hamleys.

***

Mario was the school caretaker. With his thick black drooping moustache and laughing eyes he looked every bit the Mexican bandit. Mario lived up at the school in a small apartment that had been fitted out for him. By Valle standards he lived very comfortably. He had electricity, hot running water, a bathroom, toilet and a fitted kitchen. He also had a secure job with every afternoon off. His main responsibility was to remain at the school overnight and to unlock the gates in the morning. He was occasionally called upon to do maintenance jobs and gardening. But from the beginning of his employment he showed no enthusiasm for his work.

Mondays in particular were days that Mario just could not come to terms with. Usually still drunk from his weekend revelries, he would mope about the school with a broom in his hand flicking at leaves or standing about with his shirt unbuttoned and his flies undone. On more than one occasion we had to climb over the school's perimeter fence to wake Mario up. He was an extremely likeable rogue but the idea of doing a decent day's work was anathema to him.

Alejandra Gerrard despaired of him and his ways but could never quite bring herself to dismiss him. When the time came, it took a committee decision and much discussion about his merits before he was shown the school gates: 'I know that he is useless,' she would say, 'but at least I know him!'

Mario's employment at the school lasted two years during which the flowerbeds were left unweeded, chairs and tables remained broken and unpainted and patios unswept. His busiest times were at the beginning of term when maintenance jobs left to accumulate over the previous term could usually wait no longer. But on the first day of the summer term, Mario was nowhere to be seen until Alejandra opened the door to his apartment with the spare key and discovered the caretaker in bed with two prostitutes from the neighbouring town of Colorines. Apart from various items of clothing strewn across the room, the floor was a sea of empty beer and Tequila bottles and the flat smelt of marijuana and alcohol. It was nine o'clock in the morning. An hour later Alejandra was due to show a group of prospective parents around the school. Mario had to go.

***

Valle was full of likeable rogues. *Conchita Perez* was an excellent maid. She was punctual, thorough and very polite. She was also ambitious and often took a shine to other women's husbands. Conchita worked for my neighbour, Isabel. Isabel also employed a gardener called *Ramon* who looked after the house when Isabel was away and did odd jobs. Ramon looked about 17 years old. He always wore a big black cowboy hat and boots. He lived with his common law wife in a small house at the bottom of Isabel's garden.

One day Conchita handed in her notice: 'Señora, I am getting married next week and my husband doesn't want me to work anymore,' she explained.

Isabel was sorry to see her go. Reliable maids were hard to find and Conchita had been very efficient. A few weeks later a young woman called Carmela presented herself at the door: 'I understand that you need a maid, Señora?' Carmela had said by way of an introduction. 'My little girl is three years old and I need to go back to work.'

Carmela had been recommended by a neighbour and soon started work, coming in three times a week to clean. In the meantime, Isabel had moved back to Mexico City and kept the house in Valle for weekends, with Ramon as caretaker and Carmela as maid. Several weeks passed and all seemed to be well at number 102 Culebra Street. Then one afternoon in June, I returned from school to find Carmela sitting on my doorstep in tears.

'I wonder if you can help me Señor,?' she sobbed. 'I went to the Señora's to work as usual this morning but the gate was locked. They would not let me in.'

'They' were Ramon and Conchita. Unbeknown to Carmela, Conchita had forged a letter to Isabel pretending to be Carmela. Isabel had received the message just before returning to Mexico on a Sunday evening. She had thought it very strange since Carmela had been around to clean that very morning and had said nothing of resigning. But Isabel was in a rush. Although she was upset and surprised by the note she had other things on her mind, such as the Toluca bound traffic she would shortly be sitting in. And then, just as she was packing the car, Conchita walked by looking downcast and forlorn:

'Marriage was not what I thought it would be, so I left him,' she said to Isabel. 'Now I am looking for work. I don't suppose you know anyone who needs a maid?'

And that is how Conchita got her job back. Behind the scenes Ramon and Conchita had been having an affair and when Conchita's marriage broke up she wanted to be with Ramon. The fact that Ramon had a wife was no obstacle. So the two of them had planned to get rid of Carmela whom neither of them liked and who always looked disapprovingly at them when they were together at Isabel's.

In the end Carmela got her job back and Ramon was dismissed from service. But the incident reminded me of another occasion when Ramon had spun a yarn in order to get his own way.

'Señor, will you lend me 50 pesos to go to the doctor?' He had asked me one afternoon. His arm was in a sling and he was nursing it with his free hand.

'I fell off the Señora's gate when I was fixing the bell. I think I have broken it.'

I gave him 50 pesos and never thought to doubt his story. But a few days later I heard a different tale. I had gone to the house to leave a message for Isabel.

'I see that the bell has been fixed,' I commented to Carmela in passing.

'It was never broken Señor,' replied Carmela.

'Oh! I thought Ramon broke his arm trying to mend it. Didn't he fall off the gate?'

Carmela laughed. 'Ramon didn't fall off the gate. He broke his arm when he fell off Dylan's skateboard!' Dylan was Isabel's youngest son.

***

There were other stories about Ramon and Conchita. Isabel came down one weekend to find that her bed had been slept in. There had been no visitors that week so it could only have been Ramon or Conchita, or both.

'Well Señora,' exclaimed Ramon, his eyes to the ground, his black hat held in both hands as if at a funeral.

'It happened like this. Conchita was making the bed and she, well, Señora, – she asked me to help her. How could I refuse?'

CHAPTER 28

HISTORIA

Dad says there has been a terrible earthquake in Nicaragua. Buildings collapsed and hundreds of people have been killed. Nigel Spiers' wife is from Nicaragua. There was a tremor here last week. Dad says some people at the office fell off their chairs when it happened.

***

After school one afternoon, I returned to the museum to read up on Valle's history. I found Pablo Ramos in his office. He was filing paperwork.

'You've got the place to yourself this afternoon,' he said smiling. 'I would start by looking at Castillo and Piña: I'll bring you a cup of cafe de olla in a minute.'

***

Vallesanos divide the whole of their history into two periods: *antes y después* - before and after. 'Antes' refers to Valle before the construction of the lake in 1948; the way life was stretching back to the town's foundations and by implication no longer is. 'Después' describes the new Valle, when the valley was dammed and the waters of the Temascaltepec river flooded what were once fields of corn and wild flowers and the local geography was changed forever.

The date was November 12th 1530. A small group of Franciscan monks led by Friar *Gregorio Jimenez* stopped briefly in a forest clearing to admire the view unfolding before them. In the distance about 20 leagues away a huge outcrop of rock rose out of the valley floor. Further away on the horizon rolled range after range of forested hills. The air smelt of wild flowers and dust and reminded them of home and the hills of Old *Castille*. They stood in silence panting after the steep climb.

Three days previously they had left their monastery in Toluca with instructions to establish a Christian mission and a new outpost among the Otomi and Mazahua 'savages.' They carried no maps with them nor did they have any idea where they would be spending that night but they trusted God who had brought them safely this far.

Already they had encountered adventures along the way. Only the day before, on passing through an Otomi settlement near the village of *Zinancantepec*, a two day walk from Toluca, Friar Gregorio had saved the life of a local chieftain. The old indigena had a gangrenous leg wound and none of his witchdoctors had been able to cure him of the raging infection. Friar Gregorio, who had been trained as a physician in Seville, immobilised the limb and after gathering some wild fungus made an ointment which he applied to the wound. The Franciscans remained guests of the Otomi for two nights and soon the chieftain's condition improved and the fever left him. He was so grateful to the Spaniards that he provided them with guides and an escort of 10 warriors.

A further six hours of difficult walking through dense forest brought them to the outcrop of rocks they had spotted from the heights of Zinancantepec. The Otomi knew the site well and informed the Spaniards that they had entered the land of the

Mazahua, their ancestral enemies against whom they had fought many territorial battles and with whom they shared only one thing in common; their hatred of the Aztecs.

The Otomi warned the monks against camping in the valley, but Friar Gregorio had made up his mind, that there, in the beautiful upland meadow, surrounded on all sides by steep forested mountains with its own natural fortress was where the Franciscans would establish their church.

They were in the process of setting up camp when from the west, descending through the forest, a Mazahua war party came upon them, numbering several hundred warriors. The Franciscans and their Otomi guides were ambushed and within the first few minutes of the attack, one of the monks was killed, pierced through the heart by an arrow. Other monks fled in panic; their bodies were later found in the forest, scalped and mutilated and covered in flies.

Friar Gregorio knew that they would all be slaughtered unless he attempted to stop the battle. In a defiant action that astounded and amazed both the Mazahua and Otomi warriors, Gregorio raised two swords in the air in the sign of the cross and proclaiming the Gospel in his deep, booming voice he approached the Mazahua ranks and threw himself at their cacique's feet. An eerie silence descended suddenly over the battlefield as all eyes turned towards the priest.

Soon other monks joined their leader and their Otomi allies laid down their weapons. That evening, due to the courageous actions of the priests and the extraordinary mercy demonstrated by the Mazahua, the Franciscans were permitted to camp in their midst and to found their first church. The date was the 16th September 1530 and the town which was rapidly established became known as Valle de Bravo.

***

After independence, Mexico experienced more than a century of political and social upheaval as revolutionaries and reactionary forces struggled for power, and it was small towns like Valle that suffered the most in the ensuing chaos. Valle was traditionally a conservative town but due to its geographical position between the coast and the plains, it was often the scene of bitter battles as first pro-government forces and then Zapatistas took the town.

But by far the blackest dates in Valle's history were the early years of the 20th century when raiding revolutionaries led by *Alberto Sara*, a lieutenant in *Emiliano Zapata's* army, attacked and destroyed much of Valle's colonial architecture and heritage. The worst attacks came in the summer of 1912. On June 16th at six o'clock in the morning, Sara rampaged through Valle. Fifty government soldiers tried to defend the town from the square but on seeing that they were outnumbered, they fled leaving the towns people to fend for themselves. For 10 desperate hours the people of Valle put up an heroic resistance, taking up strategic positions from rooftops, balconies and trenches as they waited for government reinforcements from Toluca. But by four o'clock in the afternoon their ammunition ran out and the bandits quickly stormed the town. All the municipal buildings, including the library, were razed and private property and homes were ransacked. Over 1,000 men, women and children were rounded up, driven into corrals and slaughtered. Valle suffered both socially and economically. Few businesses and industries were left standing and by the beginning of 1913, a mass exodus had begun as families left Valle to start new lives in the neighbouring states of Michoacan and Guerrero.

A few people remained, but Valle with its burned out buildings and empty streets, was considered a black spot on the map and passing through it was said to bring bad luck. Valle was practically a ghost town.

~

CHAPTER 29

EL MAL DE OJO

Mrs Atherton, my teacher, died whilst we were on holiday. Mum said she had lung cancer and that she was a heavy smoker. I will be going to another school now called Greengates. I have to wear a uniform and go to school by bus.

***

In early March Mark met up with an old colleague from The Edron School in Mexico City and invited her and her sister for a weekend in Valle. Just before they were due to arrive, he cycled over and asked if I could help accommodate them.

'You know my cabin,' he pleaded. 'There's barely enough room to swing a cat and apparently there are now three of them coming down; a friend has joined them, and you do have masses of space!'

'Well thanks a lot mate!' I replied slightly peeved. 'I was planning on going for a bike ride – I suppose I've got to stay in now and wait for them?'

'Come on!' implored Mark. 'Three women staying in your place for the night – it's practically a harem! Most men would jump at the opportunity.'

'I'm not most men. What are they like?'

'Well I've never met the sister or the friend but Eveleen is petite and very pretty with huge green eyes!'

'Well all right – but I am not looking after them. I'll give them a spare key and they come and go as they please. But you owe me big time – I mean big time!'

With that, Mark gave me a thumbs-up sign and cycled off to the square to meet his guests.

I had planned on cycling up towards Cerro *Gordo* and then on to *Laguna Negra*, a round trip of about three hours. Now, thanks to Mark, it wasn't going to happen. I changed back into jeans and a shirt, put on some music and returned to the roof terrace to wait for Mark and his bevy of women.

Fifteen minutes later, I heard a car approaching up the Culebra. It stopped and then I heard Mark's voice from below.

'Guests have arrived to check in at the Hotel Don Marcos,' he shouted up. I looked over the railings and saw a red Volkswagen Golf parked in front of the house and three women in sun glasses looking up expectantly.

When I opened the gate Mark introduced me.

'This is Eveleen,' he said pointing to a dark haired woman dressed in a mini skirt and sandals. 'I used to work with her up in the DF; and this is her sister Sharon and their friend Alice.'

Sharon smiled behind her sun glasses and said 'Hello,' meekly. She was fairer than her sister and dressed in a pair of mauve jeans and a short sleeved stripped top. My first impression of the sisters was how different they were. Eveleen reminded me of a rock chick. Sharon bore an uncanny resemblance to Madonna; or was it Kate Winslett? I couldn't decide.

Alice was larger than life in both personality and physique. A character from a St Trinians film came to mind. She was freckled with shoulder length hair and an open face. She wore the kind of skirt a hockey coach might wear.

Eveleen and Alice were instantly effusive, commenting on how quaint the house looked and how much character it possessed. I showed them to the spare bedrooms and left them to decide on the sleeping arrangements. When I descended to the kitchen, Mark was grinning like a Cheshire cat.

'Sorry for lumbering you with all of this. Let's go to the *Tres Arboles* and I'll buy you a beer.'

'A beer!' I exclaimed. 'Is that all? You tight arse! You can pay for my meal and I'm ordering mole *poblano* and several *micheladas* and coffee!'

***

The Tres Arboles, near the market offered Mexican Lebanese food with a difference. It was a favourite with members of the staff and we had enjoyed several lunches there over the months sitting out on the sunny terraces sipping Jamaica and agua de tamarindo.

Eveleen was very loquacious and interested to learn what life in Valle was like. Alice was more intent on finding out which schools and university I had attended. Sharon listened to the conversation but sat contentedly in silence. She intrigued me. When she finally removed her sun glasses, I spotted the sisterly resemblance to Eveleen; the similar bone structure and large animated eyes and English rose complexion. I couldn't decide whether she was painfully shy or just very haughty. I asked her one or two questions which generated mono-syllabic responses and after finishing my coffee left Mark to entertain his guests.

'We'll drop by at about six and pick you up if you want?' Mark shouted after me. 'Richard Jackson has invited us for drinks up at his place but we can trawl a few bars, if you're up to it.'

I nodded and made my way back home and spent the afternoon reading the 'English Patient' on the roof terrace.

At about half past six, I heard a knock at my gate and when I opened it I found the three girls laden down with recent purchases from the *Casa de Artesanias*, standing on my door step.

'So where's Mark?' I asked them.

'He could only tolerate so much shopping and has gone back to his cabin for a siesta,' said Eveleen laughing, 'but he will join us at about eight.'

Two hours later Mark turned up in his battered yellow Beetle. I had barely seen my visitors since they returned from their shopping spree, so focused were they in preparing for their night out in Valle but several times on passing the bathroom I was met by billowing clouds of vapour from underneath the door and surmised that the three of them must have taken lengthy showers and in doing so probably used up a month's worth of kerosene!

***

We started the evening at Balzaretti's where we had a couple of drinks before driving up to Richard's house in Avandaro.

Richard hailed from Sheffield and had originally come out to Mexico as an employee of British Steel. He married Anna, a Mexican and had two daughters and when his contract with British Steel ended the family moved down to Valle where Richard started his own construction business. He was stocky; built like a rugby scrum half and looked like the singer Joe Cocker. Anna was tall, dark and elegant.

We spent an hour or so with them snacking on *botanas* that Anna had prepared and sipping micheladas. When we left them at around eleven o'clock, Alice and Eveleen returned to the Culebra but I was surprised that Sharon chose to stay on with Mark and me as we continued on the party trail. We moved on to Elisa's for an hour taking on a few more beers and then ended up at one of Valle's two clubs on the *Costera* road. By midnight, Sharon had relaxed in our company and had become almost gregarious. Out of humour, I chose to be provocative and deliberately belligerent in order to get a reaction from her and told her (amongst other things) that I was a paid up member of the National Front and had far right views on everything from homosexuality to immigration. I fooled her for a while but she quickly cottoned on that it was all an act and began to warm to me. I was flattered that she laughed at my jokes and she found it amusing when I told her that Mark and I were going on to another party but had arranged for a donkey and an old muleteer to pick her up and take her back to my house. I was certainly warming to her, but by the end of the evening I still knew very little about her apart from the fact that she was a fine arts graduate and had been educated at a Catholic girls' school.

The following morning Eveleen, Sharon and Alice continued shopping; revisiting the market and various craft shops before meeting up with Mark and I for lunch at the lakeside and heading back to Mexico City.

I tried persuading Sharon to visit Valle again but she was very evasive and the only response she gave me was a wistful smile, a 'maybe' and a wave from the back of the car as they left Valle.

***

EL MAL DE OJO

It was Richard Jackson who told me the curious story of *Pablo Sanchez*. Pablo was a fit and healthy 25 year old with 10 years of state education behind him when he first started to work for Richard as a carpenter. Richard had been good to the Sanchez family, buying schoolbooks and clothes for Pablo's younger brothers and sisters.

Pablo was a good worker. He was punctual and a quick learner and within a short period of time had become an accomplished cabinetmaker. But one day Pablo did not arrive at work. It was to be a busy day. Richard had just begun renovating an old town house and he needed all his carpenters on the job. At eleven o'clock, Pablo's father, Victor, an elderly man with grey eyes and a moustache, arrived to apologise on his son's behalf. Pablo, he said was ill in bed with a temperature and mild facial rash. On Monday morning, however, Pablo was still confined to his bed and his fever showed no sign of diminishing. Richard insisted that he visit a local doctor and even paid for a taxi to pick the young man up. The doctor gave him a thorough medical and prescribed a course of antibiotics to treat the mild infection that had caused the rash.

All fears that Pablo's illness had been anything more serious were now allayed and it was expected that he would shortly return to work. But Pablo never did. After taking the prescribed medication for two days he discontinued the treatment and his infection worsened. His face was soon covered in boils and he lay for hours on his bed groaning and refusing to eat.

One afternoon, about a week later, Richard (who had paid Pablo's medical bills) stopped by to visit the patient. What he encountered was shocking. Pablo lay delirious in a dark corner of the tiny house. His face was a mess of oozing sores that emitted a foul, rotting smell.

'Why hasn't Pablo been taking the medication?' Richard asked Victor Sanchez in dismay, noticing half a box of penicillin on the bedside table.

The old man looked downcast and held up his hands.

'My son does not believe the medicine will make any difference to his condition. He says that he knows what the problem is and that there is only one solution.'

'What do you mean?' asked Richard who was become increasingly bewildered.

'Pablo believes that he has been cursed by a former girlfriend. He will certainly die unless he can get the *mal de ojo* lifted by a curandero.'

'If that's what he believes, then why hasn't he gone to see one?' At the mention of the word 'witchdoctor', Richard had felt like washing his hands of the whole affair. He was quite prepared to pay for the Sanchez family's medical bills, but he would have no truck with so called 'holy men.'

'It's not that simple,' replied the old man. 'You see the curandero needs all kinds of ingredients for the ceremonies he conducts to lift the curse. These cost money. We will have to sell our donkey and cow to pay for the curse to be lifted.'

Soon Victor had sold his donkey and cow but still the witchdoctor insisted that he needed more potent ingredients. Meanwhile the fungal infection had spread all over Pablo's body and the stench of his rotting flesh filled the house. Richard decided to take matters into his own hands. He took the day off work and drove out to the

Sanchez house and insisted on taking Pablo to the state hospital in Toluca, a two hour drive away. There, Pablo was immediately admitted to intensive care. But it was already too late. The infection had got into his blood stream and Pablo, who had never shown any stamina or determination in fighting his illness, was dead within two days leaving an impoverished family.

∽

CHAPTER 30
LA VIDA LOCA

We are driving through the jungle along a rutted road filled with three months rain. All the windows are down. We are hot and sweaty. Then dad slams on the brakes and asks Jason to pass him the binoculars. 'What's happened?' asks mum. Dad puts his fingers to his lips in a gesture for silence. He looks into the canopy of trees. 'I can see a jaguar!' He exclaims.

***

If ever I wished to escape my idyllic life in Valle for a rush of adrenaline and excitement, I would spend a day in Mexico City. The Federal District was dirty, polluted, smelly, dangerous, teeming with people and positively unhealthy, but it was never boring. On this occasion, I had caught an early evening bus and was in the city centre three hours later. I didn't particularly wish to spend a night in the Big Smoke, but within two months, Mark and I were due to participate in a national triathlon and I had to register my entry at the organisers' offices. I decided that I would spend the night in a cheap hotel and try to be at the Triathlon Federation when its doors opened the following morning at ten o'clock.

From the bus station I caught a taxi to *Calle Uruguay* a block away from the City Square where I found a room in the faded grandeur of the Hotel Montecarlo. It had seen better days. Once a former monastery, it had played host to D.H Lawrence and the 19th century German explorer Humboldt who later owned a house around the corner. Humboldt had once described the city as 'The most beautiful in the world' echoing the words of Bernal Diaz, Cortés' chronicler, more than four hundred years before. Sadly, over a century later I could not agree.

I was standing at the reception desk and was paying for my room when a white Nissan drove through the front entrance, down the hall past the lounge with its television blaring and into what was apparently the hotel car park. The receptionist noticed the incredulous look on my face and smiled.

'The car park entrance outside has been closed indefinitely due to a fatal accident last month but the owner insisted on providing another way in for our clients. The hotel will lose too much income otherwise! So we knocked a hole in the wall back there and built a ramp outside,' she said raising her eyebrows. The reality of Mexico City suddenly hit me. This was the city where anything could happen.

The following morning I left my hotel early and was waiting outside the offices of the Federation ready for it to open at ten o'clock. An hour later I was still standing outside the glass fronted building. The doors were locked and there was no answer from the intercom. I decided to go for some breakfast. Perhaps it would open later. I found a roadside cafe two blocks away and ordered *huevos rancheros*, a fresh orange juice and a coffee and sat in its open doors watching the city come to life. Green Volkswagen taxis sped by, shoe shine boys appeared and set up their stalls and balloon vendors walked slowly along the leafy avenues. At a quarter to 12, I returned to *Calle Pedregal* to find that the office remained closed. A window cleaner dressed in a beige boiler-suit looked down at me from a ladder.

'You've just missed them,' he laughed. 'I think they have all gone for a coffee break. The *jefe* said that he would be back in half an hour to pay me, maybe you could come back then?'

I wasn't in a mood to hang around. Someone in Valle had told me that it was also possible to register for the triathlon at a certain branch of sports shop. After a few enquiries, I learned that there was a Marti shop in a nearby shopping centre so I headed there. I was just walking up the steps towards the centre's entrance, when a mass of screaming shoppers came flooding out and ran down the steps towards me. A man with a panic stricken look on his face passed me and shouted, 'Get away from the building; there is a mad man in there with a machine gun and he is shooting everywhere!'

'There has been hold up,' screamed a woman as she ran into the traffic and flagged down a taxi.

I retreated to the safety of a newspaper stand on the opposite side of the road to see what would happen next. The owner of the stand, a pregnant woman dressed in a *huipil* was enjoying telling an audience of bystanders what she had witnessed.

'A car turned up and two men with balaclavas and machine guns got out. One of them started firing at the wall of the shopping centre – look! You can see the bullet holes over there,' and she pointed to a section of the shopping centre's wall. 'Another man grabbed a passerby by the throat and dragged him into the mall while his companion threatened anyone who came near. They must still be in there now.'

Soon a news camera team arrived and several police cars screeched to a halt outside the shopping centre. Police commando officers wearing bullet proof vests and helmets and carrying shotguns nervously approached the entrance. For five minutes nothing happened. Another passerby had seen a police team entering the mall from the underground car park. 'It will be over soon,' he added.

Shortly afterwards, the manager of the shopping centre opened the glass doors reassuringly and gave the all clear. I waited a few more moments before crossing the road and entering the mall. I had just passed MacDonald's on the left of the entrance when there was another rush for the doors and more screaming. 'They are still in here,' shouted a policeman. 'Everyone out!'

This prompted chaos as hundreds of shoppers, their arms laden with bags, headed for the exit. I ran for the cover of the nearest pillar. Other shoppers crouched behind plastic dustbins, benches and food stands in the central foyer. Two long minutes passed as hordes of people pushed and shoved their way dangerously through the doors. Two old men were pushed to the floor and almost trampled on. Everything seemed to happen in slow motion. I could feel my heart pounding against my shirt but felt curiously detached from everything. Meanwhile, young policemen barely out of the academy marched in with an arsenal of weapons and dispersed throughout the building. I could see a number of officers standing in corners anxiously clutching their shotguns. It was a scene of total confusion. I waited a couple of minutes and then decided to join a group who were making a dash for the exit. The pillar, I concluded would offer little protection against robbers intent on taking lives or hostages. Outside I ran for a taxi. But everyone else was doing the same, and taxi drivers already aware that there had been an incident at the Coyoacan shopping centre were not stopping. I changed directions and ran down *Universidad* and out of sight and soon found myself in some quiet back streets.

Half an hour later I was back at the hotel. As I was picking up my keys from the reception desk I overheard the news from the television.

'There has been a shoot-out at Centro Coyoacan,' said the newsreader soberly. One man is reported to have been killed in the incident and several wounded. After a short siege two masked gunmen gave themselves up to the police,' and the news switched swiftly over to the day's sport.

Another trip to Mexico City had been full of surprises.

***

My bus back to Valle left the following morning at 11 o'clock, which allowed me enough time for a cup of coffee in *Observatorio* Station and a quick visit to public toilets. At Observatorio – and in fact at all public conveniences, spending a penny or two was literally what you had to do if you were suddenly caught short, though where the money went and what it was spent on remained a mystery to me!

In front of the entrance to the 'gents' sat a grumpy little man with a pencil thin moustache dressed in a grubby vest. In exchange for a peso – about 20 pence, he handed me a ticket which allowed me to go through the turnstile and into the lavatories. I presumed the payment was to maintain the public conveniences, but there was no evidence of this. The grim reality was what I had come to expect of public toilets all over Mexico: graffiti everywhere, an overwhelming stench of stale urine, cubicles with no locks on the doors, overflowing latrines and scraps of used toilet paper strewn on the floor. In one cubicle, someone had not even bothered to tear bits off the roll. The whole thing had been used and left to float in the un-flushed bowl.

Outside the cubicles, a cleaner whisked a filthy mop across the floor splashing a mixture of urine, wet paper towels and dirty water over everyone's shoes. When I went to wash my hands, I discovered that the sink was blocked and I was faced with a basin full of oily black water.

I had an hour to wait before my bus left for Valle, so I sat down opposite the gents to count how many people went into the lavatory each paying a peso. By the time I had to leave, 80 men had passed through the turnstile. I did some quick calculations in the back of my notebook.

Observatorio station was open from five o'clock in the morning to midnight seven days a week. It was also one of the busiest terminals in the country with buses travelling to the Pacific Coast and other major cities. If on average 50 men used the gents in an hour, the toilet business would generate an income of about 5,600 pesos a week – approximately £1,000. But what was this money being invested in? Not in toilet paper, effective detergents or good plumbing. Someone somewhere was making a nice sum of money in an unusual sideline.

CHAPTER 31

A ZIHUATANEJO

Mr Mayberry was arrested by the police when he arrived in Acapulco. He ran over a pig passing through a village and there was blood on the bumper of his car. Earlier in the day a young girl was hit and killed by a truck. The police thought it was Mr Mayberry. He was in gaol for two weeks.

***

Two weeks after their visit to Valle, Eveleen contacted Mark and asked whether they could come down again. Alice had ordered a coffee table from a local carpenter and it was ready to pick up. Mark, of course suggested they stay at the Hotel Don Marcos. I was pleased that I would be seeing Sharon and Eveleen again but not so keen on Alice staying. On cleaning the guest bedrooms after their last visit I noticed that Alice had broken the bed. One of the legs had buckled under her considerable weight and she had failed to mention this when leaving. I suppose it would have been a bit embarrassing to have said: 'Well thank you for putting us up for the weekend but by the way, I broke your bed!' I hadn't really warmed to her, and got the impression she wanted to pigeon hole me: to her I was posh, middle class, public school and probably just like her. Little did she know that I was born in Argentina and had spent a good deal of my life outside the United Kingdom and didn't really fit into any 'class.'

***

By the end of March, Mark and I were several months into training for the National Triathlon, which was due to take place in and around Valle in June. We had been on regular bike rides and swam twice a week in addition to running in the afternoons after school. We were now planning an extended mountain bike ride through the rugged *Sierra Madre Occidental* from Valle to the fishing town of *Zihuatanejo* on the Pacific, during the Easter holidays. Keen to pursue Sharon, I had made up my mind to ask her if she was interested in meeting us down there at the end of our ride. She would of course have to make her own way down to Zihuatanejo; but what the hell! If she said, 'No!' and rejected my advances, well that would be it, I need not see her again!

Eveleen and Sharon arrived just after mid day. Fortunately, Alice had made other arrangements to stay with Isabel, who was also a colleague at The Edron School. Clearly she was embarrassed by the 'bed incident' and wished to avoid me – which wasn't such a bad thing!

Mark and I arranged for a guide to take us on a tour of the lake which lasted a couple of hours. We were taken to the foot of various spectacular waterfalls that plunged from the forests above Valle into the lake and given a potted history of the region. I learned that Sharon had come out to Mexico in October having given up her job working as a civil servant for the courts in Leeds. She had no fixed plans and had ended up working as an assistant in the art department at Edron where the young Mexican actor *Gael Garcia Bernal* was a student. She was staying with Eveleen who now lived with Juan, a former Tae Kwando instructor, near the Desierto de los Leones.

Later that evening, at a party at Rosa's house and after several beers, I asked Sharon if she was interested in meeting us in Zihuatanejo at the end of our bike ride. I was completely taken by surprise, when without reservation she said, 'Yes!' We spent the remainder of the evening planning the adventure. Mark and I thought it would take us about three days to cycle down to the coast. By bus it would only take Sharon a day, so she would find a local hotel and wait for us. We had no way of communicating with her, so Mark suggested she try and reserve rooms at the *Hotel Tres Marias*, near the river. If they didn't have rooms there, she could leave a message for us with further instructions.

***

Luis Rosas looked at us as if we were crazy. 'You really don't have to do this,' he said, his rich, smooth Mexican accent made his English sound more authoritative. 'It's not a good idea!'

I knew that our friend was probably right. We had heard nothing good about the road to Zihuatanejo that ran through the state of Guerrero. Popularly known as the 'Death Run,' the road was notorious for banditry and general lawlessness. Only a week before, highwaymen had flagged down a bus and passengers were forced to empty their wallets and purses at gunpoint into the hands of bandana masked thieves.

The local police were said to be equally corrupt. A year before, they had massacred the entire population of the small village of *Santa Cruz de la Sal*. Initial reports stated that the policemen had gone to the village in search of drugs when the villagers had attacked them. They had fired back in self defence. At a press conference a television reporter asked the state police chief why women and children had also been killed. 'Well they attacked us too,' was his response.

Only later did it emerge that although the incident had involved drugs, the facts were not as they had been presented. Two men in the village had been growing marijuana and certain corrupt police officers had offered them protection in exchange for a share of the profits. On this occasion, the officers had gone to Santa Cruz to collect their cut but the villagers refused to co-operate and attacked them with sticks and stones. In retaliation, the police lined up the 35 inhabitants of the small hamlet and shot them all.

Mark and I had been planning this ride since Christmas and had studied the route many times. Starting in Valle, in the shadow of the *Nevada de Toluca* we would descend through pine forests to *Bejucos* on the edge of *Tierra Caliente*. From there we would cycle to *Ciudad Altamirano* situated in the middle of a hot, dry plain surrounded by mountains. Then the hard work would begin; two to three days of mountain cycling through the Sierra Madre, before dropping down to the Pacific.

***

The busy term ended on the second of April. Coming home from school, I stopped at the bike shop to buy some spares: brake and gear cable, some puncture repair kits and two more water bottles. I also went to the market and bought a kilo of mixed nuts, raisins and sweets to be eaten as energy snacks along the way, and one or two items for the first aid kit. There would be just enough room in my rucksack for a change of clothing, a camera, my journal, binoculars, penknife and an all purpose sarong. I would carry my passport, work papers and my wallet in a pouch around my waist. I also hid a small cache of emergency money in the handlebars of my bike. Just before going to bed, I pumped up the tyres, oiled the chain set, filled my water bottles and put them in the freezer.

At seven the next morning Mark knocked on my gate. We were ready to go. Our first destination was Temascaltepec, 21 miles south of Valle. We cycled out of town on the Toluca road weaving through pine woods with views down to the village and across the lake. As we climbed out of Valle, a lorry came bouncing down the road towards us. As it approached I could hear loud barking from the back and as it passed, a huge German shepherd lunged over the side of the truck and tried to bite my head. I swerved to the right, my front tyre hit a sharp rock on the roadside and I fell sidewise 10 feet down a rocky ravine. As I clambered back up to the road, my knees and elbows grazed and scratched, I heard Mark's loud guffaws.

'That's a great start!' he exclaimed.

After a further three miles of cycling, Valle disappeared from view but we could still see Cerro

Gordo's round top towering over the valley. At mile post 17, we turned off the main road and headed east along a sandy, rutted road. This was blissful cycling. There was no traffic on the mud-backed track. It weaved through deciduous forest with wonderful views of the snow-capped Nevada de Toluca. Occasionally we passed campesinos in neighbouring fields and riders on horseback and mules heading into the high sierra. After half an hour's cycling, *Doctor Uribe*, passed us in his pick-up truck.

'So you decided to go?' He said with a smile. He stopped and leaned out of the window.

'You'll be fine. Most people exaggerate the dangers of this road. Keep your heads down, mind your own business and *mucho animo*!' he shouted, and drove off whipping up a cloud of dust.

***

Tarcisio Uribe was an excellent doctor with a sympathetic bedside manner. His two sons, *Tato* and *Quique* were pupils at La Escuela Valle de Bravo and we quickly discovered that we shared a number of pastimes in common including mountain biking, horse riding and tennis. The Uribes had a weekend ranch up near Cerro Gordo where they kept a flock of sheep and several horses. Tarcisio was married to Monica. Her parents were German but she had been born and brought up in Mexico. They were devout Catholics and firm supporters of the school and its philosophy.

Tarcisio set up his surgery in *Ottumba*, the poorest barrio of Valle. There were other surgeries in Valle, some practically next door to each other, but Ottumba with its shacks and polluted river into which the locals dumped their rubbish and washed their clothes was largely neglected.

Before long the surgery's steps had become something of a meeting place. Children played in its open doorway and all kinds of people stopped by to chat to *'el doctor.'*

El Cerillo – the matchstick was a frequent visitor. He looked like a Glaswegian dockworker. He was small and wizened with a head of red spiky hair. He was one of Valle's many characters. He stopped me in the street once to tell me that his wife had left him.

'Why? I don't know,' he said cheerfully. 'She had everything she needed: food, clothes and a roof over her head. What else did she want?'

Being a doctor in Ottumba was a constant challenge. One morning a man stopped by to have his finger stitched. He had severed it cutting sugar cane with a machete. After stitching it up Dr Uribe advised him. 'You need to keep that finger clean or it will become infected. And don't forget to come back here next week to have the stitches removed!'

Two weeks later the man returned. His finger was a festering mess and it appeared to be covered in a network of tiny fibres.

'What on earth have you put on it?' asked the doctor.

'Cobwebs,' the man replied. 'It's the best thing for wounds. And do you know what else is good?' the man continued. 'Piss, but not any old piss mind you; it must be boys' piss. Now can you take these stitches out, my finger hurts like crazy?'

***

We stopped for breakfast in sleepy Temascaltepec. The only place open was the market so we carried our bikes up three flights of stone steps and ordered *huevos a la Mexicana* and coffee. It was really too heavy a breakfast for a day on the road but we did not know when we might be eating our next meal.

From leafy Temascaltepec we set our sights on Bejucos, 31 miles away lying in a dusty plain on the banks of a river. We stopped frequently to take photographs of the countryside: the rolling hills, the strange shaped cacti, donkeys and stray dogs. Twenty eight miles from Temascaltepec we spotted Bejucos below us from a windy bluff in the side of a hill. As we were cycling down the fast descent, a huge mongrel darted out from a small ranchito and chased us snapping at our legs. I unhooked a spider bungee and thrashed at it, hitting it on the snout. It yelped and came to a sudden halt, giving us time to pick up pace and cycle away. The six miles descent into Bejucos was fast and exhilarating – the last of its kind for two days. Ahead lay the mountains before the final drop to the sea.

It was Palm Sunday. We found accommodation in a grubby *casa de huespedes* on the outskirts of town. Paint was peeling off its walls in great flakes, the bedding was damp and only a trickle of rusty water flowed from the shower head. When Mark pulled back his bed covers, a brown scorpion scuttled out and disappeared into the floorboards.

After paying for the room, we cycled into town. The large white church was decked in flowers and freshly cut palm leaves and there was the heavy smell of melting wax and incense. Outside, everyone was preparing for the fiesta. Stalls around the square were being set up and a wooden stage and huge black speakers were mounted beneath the town hall in preparation for the band. We bought an *agua de limon* and sat at a table under one of the colonnades. Mark spotted a cantina with a pool table and after a couple of tacos, we strode across the square and in through its swinging doors for another round of our marathon pool challenge. After almost six months, the score stood at 94 frames to 42. Mark was decisively the better player.

The next day and a half were surprisingly leisurely as we climbed up to Ciudad Altamirano, the state capital of Guerrero situated in the middle of a vast plateau. As we were leaving the town, two old women sitting in their doorways shelling almonds stopped us.

'Gringos,' they said, 'young men like you with futures ahead, should not be cycling this road. Only death and misery come to those who travel along it,' they exclaimed. 'Don't you know what lies out there between the sierra and the sea?' said one of the crones, incredulously.

'No,' we answered, though we knew what she was referring to.

'*El demonio* – the devil,' she said. 'The hills are full of bad men who prey on *inocentes*. They take away and corrupt our youths and leave their mothers to mourn for them. 'We will pray to the *Virgen de Guadalupe* for you!' they said as we cycled down the cobbled street.

***

When the climbing began, it was relentless and gruelling. On our second day out from Valle, we hit the Sierra Madre Occidental, a range of high barren mountains between the sea and the *altiplano*. Nothing grew in these hills except thorny cacti. The road was dusty, broken and pot holed and offered no shade. Lizards basked on oven baked rocks and rounding a switch-back into the sun we heard the distinct sound of a rattlesnake.

At two o'clock in the afternoon, having cycled 30 miles up endless hills in the heat of the day, we stopped, dropped our bikes by the roadside and collapsed onto the rocky embankment. Although between us we had already consumed 10 litres of water since starting out that morning, we were beginning to dehydrate again.

'I don't think I can hack much more of this!' Mark exclaimed. His voice sounded dry and hoarse.

'Me neither. There is nothing out here, and I don't know about you, but I've got hardly any water left.'

'Let's look at the map; there's got to be some kind of a settlement,' Mark said.

I removed my binoculars from my rucksack and scanned the hills. I could see nothing but desolate canyons and rock.

'Here, about two miles further on there's a track that leads to a tiny hamlet called *San Isidro*. Let's head there,' he said.

We reluctantly mounted our bikes and cycled on. After 15 minutes we turned off onto a single-track and presently came to a hut with a Coca-Cola sign hanging from rusty hinges. An old man sitting on a rocking chair under the only tree in the valley greeted us.

'What can I get you?' he asked.

We bought several bottles of ice cold mineral water and sat guzzling them in the shop's doorway.

We asked the old man if there was a school or church where we could lay our heads for the night. He said he would investigate and ambled off to find the village cacique. We found this amusing, since as yet we had seen no village. Presently, the old man returned accompanied by the cacique. He was a good looking man, probably in his late fifties, with iron grey hair, soft brown eyes and a weather beaten face. He introduced himself as *Cesar*.

'Unfortunately the school and church are closed,' he said. Both the teacher and the priest have returned to the coast, they won't be back until Easter. But you are welcome to stay with my brother in law.'

The hamlet of San Isidro was a collection of shacks and wooden huts tucked into the side of a narrow ravine below the track. We were soon introduced to his brother in law, a young man called *Nicolas*. He wore what was evidently traditional mountain dress: a broad brimmed straw hat with a black ribbon tied around the crown, tough canvas trousers, a cotton shirt and strong open huaraches.

'*Hallo!*' he said in broken English. '*You gringos? I live Los Angeles one tine,*' and he laughed revealing empty gums.

Nicolas walked us down a steep slope to an orchard by the side of a stream some distance from the road. On the way we passed his mother's house, a one room adobe hut with several pigs tied to a small fence. He introduced us to his deaf father who sat outside on an old rug staring into space.

'You can rest here until the sun goes down. I would be honoured if you would sleep on my porch tonight,' said Nicolas, smiling.

The village shop where we bought our supper resembled a broken down bus shelter with two wooden shelves. The provisions in stock amounted to three tins of sardines, a packet of stale biscuits, some tomatoes and an onion. Bottles of Coca-Cola and Sol beer lay cooling in an ice box. The owner of the stall was Nicolas' aunt, Doña *Ana*. She was a large handsome woman with a deep husky voice. She seemed to be in charge now that Cesar was no longer around and was busy directing the men of the village (all five of them) in building her a new house next to the shop. They were making adobe bricks, whilst the urchins of San Isidro surrounded our bikes and bombarded us with questions.

Doña Ana offered to make us a tomato and onion salad. She kicked a sleeping dog lying on top of a wooden chopping board under the table, wiped the board with a filthy cloth and then chopped up the salad with a rusty knife. Mixing it with the sardines we ate what seemed like the most delicious meal we had ever had!

As dusk enveloped the valley and we were making our way back to Nicolas' house, a pick-up truck rolled up outside the shop and some labourers, all friends of Doña Ana, jumped out with *machetes* and spades and ordered beers. The driver of the truck, a lean man with a dark, scarred face looked at us first with suspicion and then astonishment as we stood with our bikes.

'I do not believe you sons of bitches have been cycling in these mountains,' his face suddenly broke into a wide smile. 'Don't you know what kind of people live in these hills? Only drug dealers and killers!'

I looked around at the assembled company. None of these people fitted that description. We had been shown nothing but hospitality, but then, what does a drug dealer or a killer look like?

Nicolas and his wife laid their bedding out on the dry ground in front of the house. Their animals, a curious menagerie of pigs, dogs, chickens and two donkeys seemed to have free reign of their dwelling. It reminded me of a scene from Hugh Lofting's novel 'Dr Doolittle.' Their kitchen was a charcoal stove under a straw *palapa* outside; the toilet was a hole in the ground behind the house and the bath was an old oil drum filled with rain water.

We were offered two hammocks to sleep in which we hung from the porch. Although we had already eaten, Nicolas' wife insisted we eat again with the family and Cesar.

Supper was chunks of *chicharon* and tortillas, mushroom soup and hot cups of cafe de olla seasoned with bay leaves and cinnamon. As night fell, a single lantern hanging from a tree outside the kitchen glowed in the valley.

Cesar was in Nicolas' words, 'An educated and much travelled man.' As an itinerant butcher, he knew all the remote mountain settlements. He too warned us of bandits further south into the hills.

'My name is respected as far as the hamlet of *Condancito*, 50 leagues from here. Beyond that no one gives a damn about anything. Whatever you do, don't stop until you are over *El Paso del Infierno*.'

Keen to know exactly what these dangers were that we had been warned about, Mark and I questioned Cesar further.

'The Sierra Madre is perfect for growing Marijuana. Some of these valleys have never been mapped so drug cartels can continue their business undetected. They truck in water in the dry season, grow the weed and truck it out to the United States. Some of these cartels have better weaponry than the Federal army and certainly better than the local police, many of whom are on their payroll. These people are suspicious. If they see gringos, they immediately think of the CIA. They won't hesitate to kill or kidnap you!'

The recent assassination of a presidential candidate was still fresh in everyone's minds and a topic of conversation. As the embers continued to burn in the fire and the hills fell silent, Cesar gave us his view of Mexican politics.

'The Bill Of Rights that was recently introduced is the one good thing that this president has done. Before, the police or army would arrive out of the blue and demand money from us. If they suspected us of growing marijuana or worse; of harbouring Zapatistas, they would burn down our houses, rape our women and torture our young men without asking questions. They tortured two of my cousins last year. One night some *Federales* arrived and took the two men away. Nobody knew why. They were accused of being terrorists and supporting the movement for land reform. *Claudio* returned to the village two weeks later covered in cigarette burns. *Pancho* had his toenails ripped out and was beaten so badly that he lost an eye. Now at least, the police need to produce a warrant and they cannot raid our homes without a lawyer present.' A hopeful glint appeared in Cesar's lively eyes.

That night we did not get a wink of sleep. At various times we had pigs and several chickens clucking and snorting beneath our hammocks. A mule wandered onto the porch and Rambo, Nicolas' dog, tried repeatedly to climb into my hammock. But what prevented sleep more than anything were droning mosquitoes and

Nicolas' prized possession; a battery operated clock hanging outside the house that whistled 'The Derry Air' on the hour, throughout the night.

We were up at five the next morning. Breakfast consisted of fresh orange juice with a raw egg cracked into it.

'Believe me,' said Nicolas, 'that will keep you going all day.'

Before we left, he insisted on showing us his hunting rifle.

'Very few deer get away,' he said, proudly handing us his M16 assault rifle.

'Where the hell did you get that from?' asked Mark

'A friend of the family used to work for the *Madrigal* drug cartel and stole it from them!' Nicolas replied, laughing.

We insisted on paying the family for their hospitality, but Cesar would hear nothing of it.

'It has been a pleasure to meet you; be careful, speak to no one and keep cycling until you have passed El Infierno,' he warned us again.

We packed up, waved good bye and cycled on in trepidation.

The following three hours of cycling were the toughest so far, but we now had fresh supplies of water, the air was cool and a southerly breeze was blowing. There was no traffic and we passed few habitations and before we realized it we had cycled passed Condancito and into hostile territory, though there was nothing to indicate this.

After five hours and dizzy once again with dehydration, we cycled over El Infierno and pulled off the track at a collection of ramshackle huts, one of which sold cold drinks. A surly, dark teenage girl dressed in a cropped pink top and mini skirt, eyed us suspiciously. And then she said, 'You two are the gringo's that my uncle Cesar spoke of, aren't you?'

Mark and I were astonished. 'Yes we are,' we replied. 'How do you know?'

'My cousin drove up here last night in his pick up and told my father to look out for you. You will be safe now that you have passed El Infierno. Please, take these drinks for free!' and she smiled for the first time.

Two more hours of solitary cycling brought us to a high pass above the tree line and after ten more torturous switchbacks we reached the summit where a sea breeze greeted us. The most glorious view lay ahead: miles and miles of twisting road descended down several ravines to the canyon floor. Beyond we could almost imagine the thin blue line of the Pacific coast behind some low green hills.

*

CHAPTER 32

LA MUERTE DE LUPITA GUADARAMA

All the Mexican teenagers in Valle have motorbikes. The Braggs have bought one for Richard and Stephan. I want a motorbike. Peter Davey says that if you buy enough Hershey Bars you can win a free *moto*. Mum and dad don't want to buy lots of chocolate bars. Mum says I am too young anyway to ride a motorbike.

***

Zihuatanejo was a sleepy fishing village when I first visited it as a child back in 1970. When we arrived at eleven in the morning – hot and sweaty from our bike ride we found a town bustling with tourists. There were shops selling arts and crafts made from drift wood and sea shells and silver from Taxco. Stalls brimming over with fresh fruit lined the streets and numerous fish restaurants with tables and chairs spilling out onto the sea front were beginning to fill up.

Our immediate priority was to find Sharon. We cycled across the river to the Hotel Tres Marias but found that it was fully booked up. I asked whether a message had been left for us and the pretty doe eyed receptionist promptly produced a paper napkin on which Sharon had scribbled:

'No rooms here but have found one at the Hotel *Paraiso* in the centre of town.'

The receptionist smiled and added, 'I'll warn you, it's a bit of a dump and they cram in as many beds as they can into the rooms.'

A few minutes later we found Sharon sitting outside the hotel clad in a blue sarong and sun glasses.

'I was wondering when you two might turn up,' she said smiling. The room was indeed rather gloomy. There were three beds with no room between them and a bathroom behind a paper thin stud wall with a gap at the top of the door to the ceiling allowing little privacy.

'I tried numerous other places, but being the Easter holidays, everything is booked up! It's hardly paradise,' she said pointing to a sign with the name of the hotel on it.

By now, Mark and I were ravenous. We left our bikes in the room and walked out towards the sea front where we found a lively fish restaurant with a *marimba* band playing and ordered fish soup, *calamares* and several micheladas.

Sharon told us about her bus journey down from Mexico. 'Someone brought with them a pet iguana that managed to escape from its cage and ended up in my luggage where it ate my lunch. If that wasn't enough, I had the bus driver winking at me in the mirror the entire trip. He even offered to find me a hotel when I got off at the bus depot!'

We spent two nights in Zihuatanejo before Mark and I needed to be back in Valle for the start of the summer term. Sharon and I took a boat trip out to *La Playa de las gatas* and spent hours idling through the markets and sitting in bars watching the ebb and flow of life in the old port.

***

The bus from Zihuatanejo seemed to stop at every village and hamlet in the state of Guerrero. It was a filthy, oily looking creature that belted out clouds of black smoke. The windows were cracked and the upholstery on the seats was torn in places revealing stuffing and rusty springs. We stowed our bikes away under the bus along with chickens, sacks of maize and a consignment of straw *sombreros*.

Health and safety was not a priority on this service. Although we were fortunate enough to get seats, several people spent the entire journey to Toluca standing in the aisle and one old man crawled into the luggage rack where he promptly fell asleep. Wherever we stopped itinerant salesmen boarded the bus to sell their wares.

'Chewing gums, chocolates, peanuts, sweets, sandwiches and soft drinks,' hawked a bare chested little boy in a pair of tattered shorts.

'These pills cost only 25 pesos: they are the perfect remedy for haemorrhoids, penal warts, skin conditions and dandruff,' shouted a man in a faded linen suit and open sandals as he passed through the bus.

A barefooted indigena dressed in a brightly coloured huipil with a face like a walnut sat behind me and muttered prayers to *La Virgen de Santa Cruz* and then moaned continously for two hours.

***

As I sat gazing out of the window at the passing countryside I was reminded of a story my father once told me of a bus journey he took with a friend back in 1969 down to Chiapas.

'The bus was so packed with campesinos returning to their villages for *La Dia de la Revolucion*, we had to climb up onto the roof and sit with three other passengers on some sacks of grain.

In many ways it was more comfortable than sitting in the bus. It was a hot, humid day and the lack of air and overpowering smell of body odour was almost unbearable. At least on top of the bus there was a cool breeze and the best views of the countryside.

Outside *Puebla* our three companions got off but we were presently joined by an old man who heaved a crudely made coffin onto the roof and secured it to the sides with bits of rope. He then sat on top of it and shared two coconuts and a pineapple with us. After a couple of hours he began to feel drowsy and when we stopped in a village somewhere in Oaxaca, he took his *poncho*, laid it in the coffin and pulling the lid over him proceeded to lie down and go to sleep. He left a tiny gap at one end to allow air in but I remember thinking that he would surely suffocate. The journey continued without event until we stopped in a *Zapotec* town south of *Mitla* where two indigenas climbed onto the roof and sat on the coffin. Tom and I informed them that there was someone inside, but they spoke no Spanish and ignored us. Just as we were arriving in *San Gabriel del Rio*, the old man woke up and tried to get out of the coffin. The two Zapotecs were frightened out of their wits when their heard knocking and a muffled voice from within the casket. They believed the old man was a ghost and began screaming and shouting. Picking up their possessions and their straw hats they jumped off the top of the bus, into the river, as it slowed and came to a stop in the village!'

***

LA MUERTE DE LUPITA GUADARAMA

Back in Valle everyone was talking about the death of *Lupita Guadarama*. A wreath of flowers outside a simple shop doorway marked the spot where Lupita died. The little girl, aged six was killed on Easter Sunday when a car ploughed into her as she sat on the steps outside her home.

The driver of the battered Ford Galaxy was *Pancho Alvarez*, a morose man in his mid forties with thick curly black hair. Alvarez was drunk when he got into his car and drove at 50 miles an hour through the neighbourhood of Ottumba. A woman standing outside the *Estacion* Cafe saw Alvarez speeding by. He apparently encountered an old man with two donkeys laden with wood coming up the road towards him.

'He would have seen the woodcutter from at least 20 yards away and he had plenty of room to pass. The donkeys were walking along slowly so there was no need for what happened next,' said the woman shaking her head.

But Pancho panicked. He tried to brake but instead he rammed his foot down on the accelerator. The heavy car lunged forward out of control travelling at 60 miles an hour. Pancho closed his eyes, put his hands to his head and left the rest to the Virgin of *Guadalupe* and to fate.

'I saw him narrowly miss the man and the three donkeys. The old boy was shaken but uninjured. One of the donkeys took fright and ran past my shop shedding its load of wood on the way,' said another witness. 'Unfortunately, I did not see what happened next. My elderly mother called me inside to help her make tortillas.'

The car sped forward another 50 yards. Pancho tried desperately to regain control of the vehicle but it was too late. Instead, he drove straight into Lupita and her younger sister *Estrella*, who were sitting on the step sucking lollipops. The coroner said that Lupita had died instantly. Estrella was paralysed from the neck downwards. The impact of the car hitting the step and then the wall caused part of the roof to cave in and left a huge gaping hole in the Guadarama's white washed adobe house. Pancho was never seen again.

There were numerous theories as to what became of him. The only witness had been the muleteer but he had not wanted to get caught up in a police investigation and had vanished. Some said Pancho had in fact been killed in the crash. Others countered that he had survived but had been injured and trapped in the wreckage. It was also said that the residents of Ottumba, having been shaken from their siestas by the noise, had flocked out onto the street. Incensed by the driver's recklessness, they had pulled Pancho out of the car and in a raged frenzy had lynched him and disposed of his body. But this theory was largely discounted. *Ottumbans* were law abiding citizens and would have preferred to have seen Pancho imprisoned.

The vast majority of Vallesanos believed that Pancho had taken advantage of an arcane law still in existence in Mexico, which stated that: 'No citizen of the republic, can be prosecuted for the negligent driving of a carriage unless he is interrogated at the scene of the accident by a marshal of the law and in the presence of witnesses.'

That Pancho had been drunk whilst driving; no one was in any doubt. It was often said that if Pancho was to be found sober for more than six hours a day, then only a miracle could explain it. Neither was anyone in any doubt that the car was his. The battered Ford was his hallmark and a constant source of income for local mechanics.

Lupita was buried two days later. The whole of Ottumba attended her funeral. Her little sister Estrella was still in hospital. A week later the Guadarama's ruined house was up for sale. The family needed every penny to pay for Estrella's specialist medical care and for a wheelchair.

∽

CHAPTER 33

EL PINCHE GRINGO

We are in *Fortin de las Flores*. There are bougainvillea petals floating on the surface of the pool and thick jungle. The air is hot and humid and smells of honey suckle. A fine mist rises from the sea below.

***

Greg Rosenberg was the epitome of the American playboy abroad. With his tanned, regular good looks, his yacht, Harley Davidson motorcycle and his bachelor pad, he had it all.

Greg was the only person I knew in Valle who insisted on calling me by a different name every time I bumped into him.

'So how are you doin' Martin?' he asked me the second time we met. I was having a meal at the Monarca and he pulled up a chair and joined me.

A week later, I wandered into his outdoor recreation shop which he managed for a Mexican friend.

'Hey, good to see ya Mike,' he said, extending his hand across the counter to me.

A month later I met him walking back from the market. He was on his motor cycle and was wearing a brand new pair of aviator sunglasses.

'Say, what kinda' name is Malcolm anyway?' he asked impertinently.

Greg's landlady was also Doña Joesefina. She hated him!

'Two years ago I almost paid some local hoodlums to get rid of the son a bitch. Do you know what that *pinche* gringo did?' she said almost spitting the words out in disgust. 'He took off to the U.S for a week leaving his dog alone in the house with 7 bowls of dog food. Well the poor dog wasn't going to wait 24 hours before each meal – no, the sorry, miserable hound ate the whole lot in one day and then crapped and vomited all over the place and chewed on all my furniture!'

Greg was the kind of foreigner in Mexico who was stupid enough to carry a gun and to advertise it quite openly. Many Mexicans owned guns of one sort or another. The feisty Josefina admitted to carrying a sawn off shotgun in the glove compartment of her car. 'I'm an old lady and an easy target on the open road,' she had said to me, 'but if some punk wants to try to rob me, he'll find he's messing with the devil,' she chuckled.

Owning a gun was illegal. The punishment for a Mexican in possession of a firearm was a hefty fine and a slap on the wrist, but the police viewed foreigners with weapons in an altogether different light. A gringo with a gun carried with it all kinds of unpleasant historical connotations. A gringo with a gun was likely to spend a long time in a filthy Mexican prison. But that didn't seem to bother Greg. He was arrogant enough to think that he could get away with it.

One evening in early May, Greg was drinking and carousing in his favourite lakeside cantina. He had removed his small revolver from his ankle holster and placed it on the bar to impress the pretty barmaid, when the deputy chief of police came in for his usual shots of Tequila before going off duty. He saw the pistol on the bar but chose to ignore it and instead slapped Greg on the back and challenged him to a drinking game.

'Tell me gringo, can you handle your drink like a Mexican?' he goaded Greg. 'How about you and me have a little game?' and he ordered a line of five Tequilas each. 'If you my friend, can drink your *Tequilitas* before me then maybe I will forget the little business of your pistol. If not – well, we will have to see!'

The deputy chief of police was an overweight man in his early fifties. He had a fleshly, pocked marked face and wore a grey uniform that was far too small. His belly was practically bursting through the silver buttons of his jacket and his trousers looked uncomfortably tight around the crotch. He strutted and posed like all Mexican policemen; proud of the gun and truncheon that he carried, proud of his handcuffs and his knee length riding boots and spurs; proud of the little bit of power he wielded in a little Mexican town in the middle of nowhere.

An hour and a half later, the issue of the gun had been forgotten and the two men had moved to a table where they continued their drinking games. Both were by now well soaked. They rolled around laughing and cursing until Greg was arrogant enough to mention the gun again.

'You Mexicans are all the same – all mouth and no *cojones*! You were not really going to take my little friend away from me were you?' he slurred, pointing to his gun.

'Tell me, is that excuse for a gun actually loaded?' responded the deputy.

'See for yourself!' said Greg.

The deputy grabbed the gun and spun the chamber. He was too drunk and foolhardy to check whether there were any bullets in it but instead aimed the gun at the open fireplace and pulled the trigger. A shot exploded out of the barrel and the pistol kicked back violently in his hand. He smiled mischievously and pulled the trigger again. This time the hammer shot forward but there was just a loud click as the chamber revolved.

The deputy was no longer smiling. A menacing look came over his face. He turned the gun over in his hand and holding it by the barrel he handed it back to Greg.

'Show me that you are not a *pendejo*,' he said through his teeth, his face close up to Greg's. 'Let's play a little roulette. Gringo, you go first!'

Greg was both drunk and arrogant – a lethal combination under the circumstances. 'No, please,' he declined, 'you Mexicans are supposed to be the macho men. I couldn't possibly deny you the opportunity of proving to me what an *hombre* you are.'

'Very well,' answered the deputy snatching up the gun. He raised it slowly and stuck the barrel in his mouth. Seconds later, there was the sound of a muffled explosion. The deputy lay spread-eagled on the floor, with half his brains on the wall behind. The terrified barmaid ran out of the cantina screaming, leaving Greg and two skinny youths who had been playing pool inside.

'Man, I never saw a drunkard move so fast,' said one of the boys in a radio interview early the next morning. 'That gringo was out of there and onto his motorcycle like lightning!'

A few days later Greg's shop was boarded up and warrants for his arrest had been posted throughout the republic.

'All I can say is good luck and good riddance to him,' said Josefina. 'I sure didn't like him but I hope for his sake he made it to the border. I don't see his rich, sorry ass surviving for long in a Mexican jail.'

∽

CHAPTER 34

POPOCATEPETL

Mum and dad say that I'll have to go to boarding school next year like Jason and Lucinda. The British schools in Mexico are not very good. That means I will probably have to fly to England by myself. If I'm lucky I'll get a tin of sweets on B.O.A.C.

***

I was lying in bed early one morning when I heard the glass in the windowpanes begin to vibrate and then the metal window frames shook violently before the whole house began to sway. An external wall visibly tilted inwards, a crack appearing in the corner near the ceiling. For a moment the ludicrous thought that a truck was trying to pull the house down occurred to me. I scampered out of bed and looked out of the window and then I realised that it was an earth tremor. I shuffled on some shoes and joined my neighbours in the Culebra all of whom were now taking shelter under the lintels of their front gates.

Later in the day, I drove out of Valle to the neighbouring town of Zacazonapan. Vast swathes of the road had completely disappeared off the hillsides and others had great chasms running through them. Trees were uprooted, power lines were down and houses built of adobe were reduced to rubble.

***

On September 19th 1985, a catastrophic earthquake measuring 8.1 on the Richter scale hit Mexico City killing approximately 10,000 people. The quake caused between three and four billion dollars in damages as 412 buildings collapsed and another 3,124 were so badly weakened, they had to be demolished. The high fatality rate was partly due to the fact that the president *Miguel de la Madrid* ordered a press blackout and did not personally respond to the situation for 48 hours. Emergency services were slow to respond as were the international aid agencies and the areas worse hit were the poor suburbs and shanties where housing was not built to withstand earthquakes.

***

In 1943 near the village of Paricutin, Michoacan state, a farmer was ploughing his field when a volcanic fissure appeared metres in front of him exposing molten lava. Moments later he witnessed a huge eruption of stone and ash and the birth of a new mountain. The volcano continued growing for about a month reaching a height of 9,186 feet and the ash that rained down buried the local town and displaced a whole community.

Mexico lies on volatile ground. The city is overshadowed by the mighty Popo which at 17,802 feet remains active and a constant threat to one of the largest metropolitan areas in the world.

***

As the summer term progressed, Sharon's visits to Valle became more frequent and by midterm she was catching the early evening bus down from Mexico every Friday after school.

Before long she had transformed my stark bachelor pad into a veritable casa de Artesanias. Every weekend she would arrive with a bundle of colourful arts and crafts: rugs from Oaxaca, bright tapestries from *Jalisco*, bark paintings, masks made from coconuts, pewter picture frames, baskets, garish trays and coasters and *papel picado*. We spent a weekend painting the interior of the house pale avocado green and Sharon decorated my huge ugly fridge with a lacquered *Tamayo* print. We made lamp shades from old tin cans. We visited the market and bought colourful jugs, vases, beer tumblers and wine glasses.

Often I would get up early on Saturday morning and go for a bike ride with Mark, leaving Sharon to browse around Valle. Returning at midday, we would lunch at the market or at one of the lakeside fish restaurants.

By late May, Mark and I were ready for the national triathlon that was due to take place in and around the town at the beginning of June. For almost six months we had swum, run and cycled every week, gradually increasing the distance and our stamina. The triathlon consisted of a one and a half mile swim around buoys in the lake followed by a 25 mile bike ride and a 6 mile run. It promised to be a huge event with participants coming from all over the republic as well as from abroad.

'It will feel like a carnival,' a local organiser informed me.

To break the monotony of our weekly training schedule, Mark and I planned to climb Popocatepetl, Mexico's second highest volcano. The altitude and relentless slog to the summit would determine how fit we really were. We planned to go up to Mexico City early one Saturday morning before making our way up to the lower slopes of the mountain to acclimatise. We would then rise at dawn on the Sunday to begin the climb.

***

Catching the six o'clock bus to Mexico City, I had arranged to meet Sharon for breakfast before heading up to *Amecameca* to join Mark. As I sat on the bus and looked out of the window as it weaved its way through pine woods and then open fields where Mazahua women laid out their washing on magueys, I made a momentous decision. At breakfast, I would ask Sharon to marry me.

Since meeting her back in March, I had only seen her at weekends but I had no doubt that she was the person I wanted to spend the rest of my life with.

Sharon met me at Observatorio bus station and we found a quiet cafe a stone's throw away from the zocalo that was serving breakfast. When there was a lull in the conversation I made my proposal. I didn't go down on bended knee, nor did I have a rose or ring to give to her or a carefully prepared speech. The waitress had just refilled our *cafe Americano's* when I popped the question. There was a brief, pregnant silence, and then to my delight and astonishment, Sharon smiled and said, 'Yes!'

***

We rose at dawn and quietly closed the door to the *Tlamacas* refuge at the foot of the climb. Below us, like a treasure chest, sparkled the myriad lights of Mexico City stretching as far as the eye could see. In our torch beams we found the path banked by walls of frozen snow and began climbing. With our heavy packs it took us a while to get accustomed to the thin air and the steep gradient of the slope but eventually we established a methodical, steady rhythmic pace, stopping every 20 minutes to catch our breath.

After an hour of slow progress the pink sun rose behind Ixtazihuatl and in the distance we could see *Orizaba's* snow capped top.

Popo, like Japan's Mount Fuji, is an iconic volcano – the kind of mountain a young child might draw, devoid of details, of valleys, gullies or ridges. Its two dimensional flanks rise steeply up to the crater rim. It's a beautiful mountain to behold from a distance, rising above the Valley of Mexico, smoking peacefully, but climbing it is monotonous – a mere test of stamina, with only spectacular views of the capital and *Puebla* to relieve the drudgery.

As I trudged on and up through the crisp snow, a white dog passed me, and with its tongue lolling out of its mouth, it turned and waited. I looked around to see if its owner was coming up behind but could only see Mark some 200 yards below. I patted the dog and it followed me, sometimes running on ahead and waiting for me. I marvelled at the ease and grace with which it ran up the steep endless path with such evident enjoyment.

After three hours of climbing the snow changed to ice. We stopped and put on our crampons and took out our ice axes. Mark looked pale and exhausted but remained cheerful. 'Remind me why we are doing this?' he said and laughed. After a further three hours of climbing on hard ice I reached the crater rim and could see Popo's summit above me no more than 400 yards away. I looked into the crater, but there was nothing to see but a thin plume of sulphurous smoke and boulders. Below I could see that Mark had stopped and was slumped by the side of the trail. I waited a few minutes breathing laboriously in the cold air. The sun was now high in the sky and I felt as though the whole of Mexico lay at my feet!

When Mark showed no signs of moving I decided to climb down to him. I was disappointed not to have made it to the summit but could see that Mark was in trouble. Descending the steep ice was a lot more challenging than climbing up but I reached him in 40 minutes cutting footsteps into the ice with my axe. His head was in his hands and he looked pale and sweaty and complained of a severe headache. The altitude was clearly having an effect on him. I knew that we needed to descend to lower elevations as quickly as possible. Mark staggered to his feet and weaved about like a drunkard. Progress down the mountain was painfully slow as Mark had to stop frequently to rest but within six hours we made it back to the refuge and Mark's symptoms had all but gone. He was exhausted and took to his sleeping bag for several hours.

While Mark was resting, I sat in the evening sun on the terrace and read the mountain log. It was then that I noticed that my companion, the friendly white dog, was no longer with me. As I read the various entries I was intrigued to find several that mentioned sightings of a dog on Popo. One American climber's experience was almost identical to mine:

'Two hours after starting out I was joined by a white dog that accompanied me all the way to the crater. I stopped for a rest and a snack but when I resumed my climb to the summit the dog had disappeared. I wonder if anyone else has seen it?'

Further back in the log a Mexican hiker had written:

'They say there is a ghost of a dog on the mountain. The legend goes that back in the days of Emperor Maximilian, a Spaniard was killed on Popo when he fell into the crater. He was accompanied by his dog and the hound remained on the volcano for his master's return.'

I was pretty sure that the dog that I had seen was not a ghost! He was flesh and blood – I had patted him and felt his hot breath on my hand and anyway I didn't believe in ghosts. But I was intrigued. Where had the dog come from and where had he gone?

∽

CHAPTER 35

ABEJAS

My eyes and skin have turned yellow. The doctor told mum that I have got hepatitis. I must stay in bed and drink lots of lemonade.

***

One Thursday morning in early June, whilst I was on gate duty, I noticed that *Pedro (el pescador)* the father of one our pupils was wrapped from head to toe in bandages as he sat at the back of the car. I wondered if it was a joke, and whether he might turn up later dressed as a mummy to frighten the kids but after a few enquiries, I discovered what had happened to him.

Pedro's family owned the Tres Arboles restaurant up near the market but he was a fishmonger by trade. Pedro was a big man with boot polish stubble and a huge appetite for alcohol. It was said that no one had ever beaten him in a drinking challenge. He reminded me of Bluto, Popeye's arch enemy and he was built like an ox.

At the weekend Pedro and a friend called Pua had accompanied Mochis on a walk through the sierra. The objective of the expedition was to spot a golden eagle and to catch a rattlesnake, which Mochis swore was more delicious than any beefsteak and was best eaten with wild artichokes, thyme and other mountain herbs.

Pua was a true eccentric. Named after the initials of a socialist faction that had fought against General Franco in the Spanish Civil War, he modelled himself on Salvador Dali. An architect by profession, he liked to wax and sculpture his moustache into strange shapes and seemed to live in his broad Tilley hat and knee length riding boots. His conversation could be somewhat surreal too. The first time I met him I was standing in a queue at the bank. He did not so much as introduce himself as launch into a diatribe about his one and only visit to London.

'So you are the *Lerndener* they have told me all about,' was how he started. 'I was in *Lerdern* one time. I went into zis perb. It was a crowded perb.

I climbed onto ze bar and zen I shouted Long Fuck ze Queen! Foorshunately for me, it was an Irish perb!'

***

The three men set off on their trek early in the afternoon. A friend of Mochis' took them as far as El Pinal in his pickup truck and from there they walked towards *El Diente del Diablo*, a barren peak that rose from the pine forests below and marked the border between the temperate hills of Valle and *tierra caliente* – the hot lands that lay to the south. Between them they carried equipment and supplies for two nights in the bush: several chorizos, water, a first aid kit that included adrenaline injections and anti snake venom, sleeping bags, climbing equipment and two machetes. Mochis would build them a basic shelter using canes and maguey leaves and they would sleep out under the stars.

They had been walking for three hours and were looking for a suitable place to camp in a grove of almond trees when they disturbed a bee's nest hanging in some branches. Within seconds the swarm of angry bees was upon them. Pua managed to escape into an open meadow with only a few stings to his arms and face, but both Mochis and Pedro were covered in bees. Mochis quickly shed his rucksack realizing that the bees were probably attracted to the smell of *turon* that he had packed. Once free of his load he tried to pull Pedro's pack off his back but the frenzied bees drove him away.

'Pedro!' he shouted through the cacophony of wild buzzing and Pedro's agonising screams. 'Get out of the grove and run for the river!' A small tributary of the Temascaltepec River lay within 20 metres of them. Pedro was not only carrying a heavy pack but he was also overweight and he had been stung so many times that he was beginning to lose consciousness. Somehow he summoned the stamina to move and while Pua and Mochis watched, knowing they could do nothing for their friend. Pedro made it to the river and threw himself in. With so much weight on his back, he sunk straight to the bottom. Pua and Mochis sprinted desperately as Pedro was swept down stream. On reaching the bank, both men dived in. With what must have seemed like superhuman strength, the two friends dragged Pedro out of the water and onto the sandy bank. They were sure he was dead. He certainly wasn't breathing. They rolled the big man onto his back and checked for a pulse. There wasn't one. While Pua performed mouth to mouth resuscitation, Mochis tried to get Pedro's heart pumping again. After several attempts of cardiopulmonary resuscitation, Pedro suddenly spluttered violently and vomited up a huge quantity of water. He was breathing again and they felt a very faint pulse. But he was still unconscious. They put him into the recovery position and fell back onto the bank exhausted.

'Pua,' Mochis said gravely, 'we have to get Pedro to a doctor soon or he'll die. You and I are going to have to carry or drag him back up the hill to the track that leads to San Pedro Tenayac. From there, maybe somebody will give us a lift to Valle.'

Before they tried lifting Pedro, Mochis injected their supply of adrenaline into him.

'Too much will kill the bastard, but enough may just keep him alive,' he said.

They abandoned all their equipment except for their water bottles and the first aid kit. Pedro, they quickly discovered was far too heavy to carry.

'We have no choice,' said Pua, 'we will have to drag him; at least he is unconscious and shouldn't feel anything.'

They tied some rope into a harness and pulled it under Pedro's arms and across his chest. They then wrapped his legs and chest with spare clothing for added protection. With the other end of the rope they tied two bowlines to form a crude yoke.

For five hours they dragged Pedro up the mountain slope, over rocks and through the brush and chaparral. Every 20 minutes they stopped to check his pulse and breathing. They did not recognise their friend. His head and body were massively swollen and he was bleeding from hundreds of bee stings and from cuts and open wounds on his legs, arms and face. At one o'clock in the morning they stumbled into San Pedro Tenayac. The village was silent save for a donkey braying in a nearby field.

Leaving Pua with Pedro who lay in the dusty road, Mochis went banging on every door until a sleepy eyed young man in his underpants opened one.

'We urgently need help. My friend is dying and we need to get him back to Valle as soon as possible. Do you know anyone who can take us or lend us a vehicle?'

'The young man nodded silently, went back into the house and came out a few minutes later with a pair of trousers on and some keys in his hand.

'I'll take you. I've got a truck, but you'll have to pay for the petrol.'

The young man drove like the wind up through the mountains, fording rivers and down the dusty tracks towards El Pinal. Valle was almost in sight.

'Don't take us into town,' said Mochis. 'The best doctor in Valle has a weekend house at *El Rancho la Paloma* – it's about five minutes from here. I'll direct you.'

As luck would have it, Doctor Uribe was at home. They dragged Pedro into the sitting room and onto the sofa. Dr Uribe cut all his clothes off with a pair of surgical scissors and covered Pedro's body with a thick anti histamine ointment used for treating cattle ticks. Uribe then gave him a heavy dose of morphine and called the air ambulance from Toluca.

'We've got about an hour,' he told the two friends. 'I'm cashing in a favour. They will not normally use the helicopter as far out as this unless the president himself is dying. But they owe me one!'

***

Pedro lived to tell the tale. He had been stung over 1000 times. Due to the thick canvass shirt and trousers he had been wearing, many stings had only just penetrated his skin.

'Ironically,' said Mochis a few days after Pedro was out of hospital, 'the rucksack probably saved his life even though he almost drowned. Had he been stung in the back, he would not have lived to drink another bottle of his precious Tequila.' Neither Pua nor Mochis were religious men, but both confessed that Pedro should not have survived. 'It was a miracle,' said Pua. 'Someone up there really loves that fish smelling son of a bitch!'

༄

CHAPTER 36

EL TRIATHLON

We went on a school camp to *Campo de Mexico* at the weekend. Mr Gephardt, the art teacher played with us in the woods and helped us make bows and arrows. At night he asked me if I was homesick and if I wanted to get into bed with him. I said no and cuddled Snoopy all night.

***

'You cannot possibly wear those!' exclaimed Sharon as I stood with my white shorts on gathering up my kit for the triathlon.

It was seven o'clock in the morning and in an hour's time I would be diving into the lake for the start of the race.

'Why not? They are light, they dry easily and I can swim, cycle and run in them,' I replied.

'For a start when they're wet they'll be see through and secondly they show every bulge and contour of your nether regions. If you wear those – don't expect to see me at the finishing line.'

The truth was I had nothing else. My swimming trunks were not suitable for running in and my cycling shorts were not suitable for swimming in. I was stumped.

And then Sharon appeared in the bedroom doorway holding up a pair of green bikini bottoms.

'If you insist on wearing those revolting things then at least wear something underneath them,' and she threw the bikini bottoms on the bed.

'I can't wear your bikini bottoms – they won't fit me – and I'll look like a complete prat!'

'Believe me,' interrupted Sharon, 'You really will look like a prat if you wear those shorts – you might as well not bother wearing anything at all!'

In the end I had no choice. No one would notice what I was wearing when I was in the water and once on the bike the bikini bottoms would be concealed. By the time I came to do the run, I'd be beyond caring anyway.

***

The international triathlon took place every year in and around Valle. On average 1000 competitors took part ranging from the professional elite class to amateurs like Mark and I. There were separate categories for men, women and juniors and each category was split into age groups. We were competing in the 18 to 30 group along with 250 others. The swimming component consisted of one and a half miles of open water between buoys in the northern end of the lake. Here the water was murky, tepid and polluted with petrol from speedboats and jet skis. Despite feeling confident about my level of stamina and my ability to complete the distance, I didn't think we would do well. Both Mark and I were at a distinct disadvantage in the cycling event because we had mountain bikes unlike the majority of other competitors who would have racers. We had changed our tyres to smooth road rubbers but our bikes were still heavy and cumbersome in comparison and on the 12 and a half mile climb out of Valle, other participants would glide by.

***

The hamlet of *San Gaspar* felt like a beach party by the time the taxi dropped me off with my bike 15 minutes before the start of the triathlon. Huge loud speakers were blasting out 'Sweet Child of Mine,' by Guns and Roses, and there were stalls selling triathlon equipment and tables set out with water and other refreshments. There must have been 3000 people assembled there that morning including marshals, event organisers, competitors and spectators. Even at eight o'clock, the day was heating up. I found Mark applying Vaseline to his groin and upper thighs and asked him what on earth he was doing. 'I'll get terrible chaffing otherwise,' he said laughing. Lesley, his girlfriend whom I hadn't seen for months was busily organising his gear and chatting to old friends. We had to laugh. Standing there with our mountain bikes we looked like the comedy act. There was me with my white Lycra shorts over a pair of Sharon's green bikini bottoms and Mark with a four cornered handkerchief on his head wearing a frayed pair of jean shorts. We were surrounded by serious looking athletes clad in hydrodynamic tri-suits with their feather light racing bikes. They were munching on high energy snacks that packed thousands of calories and were swilling down glucose-rich drinks from sleek silver water bottles.

'So what did you have for breakfast?' asked Mark smiling.

'A bowl of cornflakes and a cup of tea. And you?'

'Pretty much the same,' he said and then exclaimed, 'Sod it! Who cares if we come in last – we are here to take part and to complete the damn thing. We are not in competition with these pricks – aim low is my motto!'

I had to agree. There were triathletes gathered at San Gaspar from the U.S, Great Britain – even from as far away as Australia and South Africa. It was easy to feel intimidated by their brashness, their expensive equipment and their talk of lap ratios and past records. As the klaxon blasted for the start of the race, Mark and I prised on our swimming caps, shook hands and gave each other a thumbs-up sign before diving into the brown waters of the lake.

***

In the first few minutes of the race I couldn't swim for the crowds of competitors trying to get out into the open lake. And then gradually after taking on several mouthfuls of bitter water I got into a steady rhythm of front crawl. With the first buoy in sight, bobbing up and down on the waves, I soon became oblivious to everything around me but the sound of the water lapping against my head and my breathing. Occasionally I was aware of other swimmers as they passed me but my mind remained focused. Within no time I had reached the first buoy and was turning towards the second. As my head came briefly out of the water, I could hear cheers and shouting from the shore and then it seemed I was heading for the last buoy and swimming the final 300 yards to the beach. My feet felt soft sand and then I was standing ankle deep in lake mud and running for the bike racks. A marshal (who owned a sports shop in town) recognised me and shouted, 'You're coming 16th – keep it up!' I ditched my swimming cap and goggles, put on a T-shirt, grabbed my bike, and began the 12 and a half mile climb out of Valle to Donato Guerra. Within a few minutes the heat was intense and I was drying out. Two cyclists on road bikes raced by and for a few minutes I cycled alone pacing myself up the hairpin turns. And then streams of riders shot past and were out of sight. At this point I was still counting, determined to keep track of my position, but soon after the twentieth cyclists passed me I began to lose count and decided to focus instead on my own race and performance. Time passed slowly, my water ran out and I began to feel cramps creeping into my shins, and then I crested a climb and saw marshals standing at the turnoff. I pedalled hard, changed gear and was soon starting the heady descent back towards the lake. The forest sped by, I leant low over my handlebar extensions and pedalled like a demon and was soon heading through San Gaspar back to the beach. I racked up my bike, grabbed a bottle of water and a Snicker bar and started the six mile run. That's when I felt the exhaustion hit me and my blood sugar plummet. My leg muscles felt heavy and waves of nausea swept over me. I was ready to give up. It took considerable mental effort to maintain a steady running pace and the only way I knew I could complete the race was to focus on an object, run towards it and set my eye on the next one. Sometimes it was a lamp post; other times a rocky outcrop above the road or a boat moored on the lake. Runners streaked passed me but nothing mattered now; I just wanted to finish, to sit down and drink bottle after bottle of water. When the end came, I was deliriously happy. I could see the finishing banner ahead and spotted Sharon waving and smiling and then it was over and I was dripping with sweat and shivering with cold all at the same time.

***

When I met Sharon she had bad news for me. She had bumped into Alice wandering around the market earlier in the day and had invited her and her boyfriend Brian to stay the night. They were even there in San Gaspar to watch the triathlon and meet Mark and me at the finish.

'Great,' I moaned, 'I was hoping that you and I might go out for a quiet meal this evening – I'm really not in the mood for socialising; I'm just a little bit tired.'

'I'm really sorry – they kind of invited themselves and I couldn't really say no. I can't let them stay in some grotty pension!'

Just then, Alice came bouncing through the crowd like a happy St Bernard, her boyfriend Brian in tow.

'Brian wants to cycle back to Valle and has borrowed Mark's bike,' she said. 'So I said I would accompany him on yours – if that's all right?'

I didn't have the energy to protest or to tell her that I thought she was both presumptuous and rude, and Sharon and I were planning on getting a taxi back to the Culebra anyway. By now I was ravenous so we took a detour and stopped at the Estacion for a plate of tacos and several cold drinks. When we finally got back to the house after four o'clock in the afternoon, I found that the front tyre of my bike was flat and Alice and Brian had helped themselves to beers from the fridge and were sitting comfortably in the sitting room munching through a bowl of crisps.

'Hope you don't mind,' said Alice, grinning inanely. 'We feel so at home here!'

CHAPTER 37
LA CARRETERA

We have another cat. We have called her Bellas Artes. She's completely wild and brings dead lizards and mice into the house as gifts. The only person she will allow to stroke her is Adela.

***

After the triathlon I was able to spend more time with Sharon. We borrowed the Blackmores' Volswagen Beetle and explored the State of Mexico and further afield at weekends. The 1972 *bocho* with its frayed upholsterty, its dents and rusting bumpers didn't look like a car that was going anywhere. It possessed no frills, not even seat belts and the first time we took it out we were caught in a torrential downpour and quickly discovered that the windscreen wipers didn't work. It was no beauty either and French navy blue was not a colour I would have chosen for any car but the bocho was full of character and there wasn't another car like it on the streets of Valle. After a service and with a full tank of petrol it could top speeds of 60 miles an hour.

***

Driving in Mexico can be a hazardous pursuit. The majority of Mexicans drive without a licence or insurance and many of the vehicles on the highway are not roadworthy! There are no breakdown services, villages and towns can be few and far between and Mexican drivers are prone to taking incredible risks. They will overtake on hills, and on blind mountainous bends; they will drive so close to your rear bumper that even braking slightly will lead to a crash. They don't indicate when turning and they will drive up one way streets in order to take a short cut. In the countryside, the buses are crowded and weighed down and passengers scramble onto the roofs for a ride. Open pickup trucks travel for miles on fast moving highways with children crowded into the back, and in cities mini buses bursting with commuters jostle in and out of the hectic traffic at break neck speeds. And then there is the Mexican police to contend with. The police in Mexico are notoriously corrupt.

Badly paid junior officers are coerced into paying their superiors a cut of their wages in return for promotion or preferential jobs and positions and this abuse of power goes right to the top. Many policemen are in the pay of drug cartels, particularly in the northern states that border the U.S and they supplement their meagre salaries by imposing fines and crippling bureaucracy.

Miguel Castaños, a local green grocer was driving to Toluca one night when he was pulled over by the highway patrol and told to get out of his vehicle.

'You are driving without your lights on, Señor,' said the officer.

'What do you mean?' responded Miguel. 'Can't you see, they're on!' he said pointing to the beam of light illuminating the hard shoulder.

The officer slowly removed his truncheon and standing on the bumper he smashed one of the lights.

'I think you will find that one of your lights is not working Señor,' said the officer menacingly. 'But if you pay the 50 peso fine, I will permit you to drive on to the next town where you can get it fixed.'

***

On our drives through the Republic, Sharon and I had various 'road experiences'. On one of our first excursion out of Valle we drove up towards Laguna Negra and spotting an elusive track that seemed to drop south towards the town of Zacazonapan, we decided to take it. Within minutes of beginning our descent we knew we had made a mistake. The surface of the road deteriorated dramatically and dropped steeply to the right over the side of a canyon. It was so uneven and eroded that sometimes my side of the car was inclined at an angle above Sharon and we were practically driving on two wheels. The rains had carved deep furrows down the sides of the track leaving a bank of mud and rock in the middle which grated against the bottom of the car and threatened to break the chassis in half. Unfortunately we were forced to continue. There was nowhere to turn around and the road was too steep to reverse up. After a nail biting 30 minutes we reached the bottom of the hill and drove into sleepy Zacazonapan.

***

Driving to *Patzcuaro* at the end of June we came to an abrupt stop where a river had broken its banks and had flooded the road. There was a deep, muddy pool about 15 feet wide before the road continued on the other side. Looking at Sharon I asked her, 'What do we do now? If we turn around we will have to go the long way via Donata Guerra – it will add a further three hours to the trip.'

'Let's drive through it!' was Sharon's reply.

'Why don't we see how deep it is first?' I got out of the car and found a long stick in the grass by the side of the road. Approaching the pool, I leant out over it as far as I could and stuck the branch into the water until it touched the bottom. The height of the water measured about 40 centimetres. The water would probably come up to the level of the door but there was no knowing how deep it was in the middle. Putting the car into first gear I slowly drove into the pool. We watched as the water rose to the door and started trickling in. I pushed the car into second gear and then spurred the bocho through the rising water until we were in the middle of the pool and then out the other side onto the dry tarmac.

After a night in *Zitacuaro* we drove along the highway towards Morelia in the state of Michoacan. For hours we seemed to be the only car on the road but we were shocked by the number of animal carcasses that littered the carriageway. By the time we reached the turn off for Patzcuaro, Sharon had counted 30 'road kills' including a horse, a calf, numerous dogs, several cats a possum and a snake!

***

Returning from *Taxco* on the Toluca bound road one weekend, we got stuck behind a pickup truck pulling an enormous trailer stacked high with crates of soft drinks. It was travelling at 25 miles an hour up a steep winding road and drivers behind us in their Chevrolet Suburbans and Cherokee Jeeps were banging on their horns and itching to overtake. One by one, a steady stream of cars passed us on a blind bend, one narrowly missing a head on collision with a cement lorry. For five miles we kept our distance behind the truck as it snaked its way slowly up through the forest until the woods opened up onto a wide, open plateau. Fearing we might be crushed if the trailer or its load broke away from the truck, I put my foot on the accelerator and overtook it. Just as the truck was cresting the top of the hill, it turned too sharply into the bend and jack knifed the trailer. The driver and his companion got out just before the trailer tipped to one side and dispatched its cargo down a ravine. As I looked back through the rear mirror, I saw the two men laughing hysterically as they pointed down over the side of the cliff.

***

In Mexico it's not just the drivers and the roads that can be dangerous. You have to look out for careless pedestrians too. Driving back from Amanalco one Saturday afternoon along a dead straight road, I could see a young woman carrying a bucket with a young boy standing by the side of the road some 300 yards ahead. The bocho emitted a distinct purring sound and we were the only car on the road on a clear day, so unless the woman was both deaf and blind she would have been aware of of the car approaching. I maintained my speed travelling at about 40 miles an hour, when just as I was about level with her, she stepped out into the road. I didn't have time to use the horn. I slammed on the brakes and swerved to avoid hitting her. The edge of the bumper nicked the bucket she was carrying and knocked her sideways as we careered off the road and down a grassy embankment. Getting out of the car, I was relieved to find that both the girl and the boy were back on their feet again and were dusting themselves down. At that point, I lost my temper and shouted at them.

'What the hell were you doing? I could have killed you! Didn't you see or hear us coming?'

The woman didn't answer. She took the young boy by the hand and walked away towards some adobe huts in the trees.

***

In 1976, when we were returning to Mexico City from Puebla we passed the scene of an horrific road accident. For over an hour we had crept up a steep hillside above the city behind a huge line of traffic. When we came to a standstill and everyone switched off their engines, my father got out of the car and asked a highway patrol officer what had happened.

A container lorry was overtaking another articulated truck on the hill when it was hit by a Pemex petrol tanker. The tanker exploded on impact blowing the other two trucks off the road. Five people were killed and there were no survivors. The accident had happened at seven o'clock that morning, almost 12 hours before but when we eventually passed the scene of the crash, firemen were still trying to put out the fire and there were body bags lining the hard shoulder.

***

Our road experiences in Mexico were not always bad however. When Sharon and I were driving back from San Pedro Tenayac along a dusty track we hit a sharp metal object and punctured a front tyre. We limped on to the village of Cerro Gordo and after making some enquiries found a truck driver who helped us change the tyre and got us back on the road. Our jack was broken and the bolts securing the wheel to the axle had been practically welded on and would not yield to any of the tools we were carrying. As we waited for the tyre to be changed, the children of the village gathered around and chatted to us and a woman came out of her house and offered us a basket of prickly pears. The helpful truck driver refused any payment.

Although distance between places can be huge in Mexico, getting something to eat when you are on the road is rarely a problem. From roadside stalls selling slices of watermelon and chunks of fresh pineapple to more elaborate open air eateries serving tacos, roast chickens, tamales and soups, food is never far away. Mexicans love eating and will make numerous stops on long journeys to sample regional specialities or to buy tortillas and drink cool aguas frescas. They will sit for hours with friends and family procrastinating over whether to get back into their sweltering hot cars and resume their journeys. On trips to the beach with Sharon, Eveleen and her partner Juan we feasted on freshly caught tuna, salad and fish soup. Driving to Mexico we would stop outside Toluca for mushroom soup and quesadillas and outside Zacazonapan we regularly broke our journeys for a steak and a jug of fresh orange juice.

∽

CHAPTER 38
LA COPA MUNDIAL

Pancho went missing last week. We found him tied to an old pipe in a derelict house up the road. Alberto heard him barking. He said some builders must have caught him. Dad's away in Pittsburgh so Mum called Johnny Serpell. He climbed over the wall and rescued Pancho

***

World cup fever gripped Mexico in mid June and there was an air of optimism in Valle that was almost tangible. The nation's hero was the diminutive goalkeeper and captain *Jorge Campos*, who dressed like a medieval court jester with antics to match. At five feet six inches tall, he was the shortest goalkeeper ever to play in the World Cup and at the time was ranked the second best keeper in the world after the Danish footballer, Schmeichel. Every boy in the school wanted to play goalkeeper during break time and there was only one goalkeeper they wanted to be: Jorge Campos.

On the 19th of June, Mexico played its first match against Norway. All classes were suspended and Alejandra Gerrard brought her widescreen television in (a rarity then) and the whole school assembled in the largest classroom to watch the match. Norway narrowly won but Mexico went on to beat Ireland and later drew with Italy which sent them through to the last 16. On hearing the news that the national side had got through the group stages to the quarter finals, a feeling of fiesta swept through the school and even the girls wanted to play football. The end of term was still a month away but the children abandoned all thought of school work. Football mania had taken over and when the children weren't kicking footballs around, practising their kick-ups or cartwheeling like Jorge Campos, the topic of conversation was all about football: who had scored the most goals, who was the world's best striker and whether Mexico would win.

***

Everyone wanted to be out playing sport and after school, parents began gathering on the basketball court to knock a volleyball around. First it was an enthusiastic dozen; parents who arrived early to pick up their children and so spent an idle ten minutes or so in play. But the game quickly gained interest and momentum and soon up to 30 parents were staying on after three o'clock for an hour or so of hotly contested volleyball.

There were amateurs like Mark and I who had never played before and then there were the serious players who contested every point as if their life depended on it and cursed their teammates when they slipped up. *Sergio* the owner of *Los Churros* restaurant was one such parent. He had briefly been a professional tennis player in his youth and even in his early 50's was an agile athlete. His speciality was the moon serve – a ball punched vertically 20 or 30 feet high that dropped on the opposing team like a bomb and was almost impossible to control.

It wasn't just the men who were competitive: half the players were women who had dabbled at volleyball in their youth and were re-discovering the sport. Whilst their parents played volleyball, the children watched the World Cup highlights on Alejandra's television or played football on the small pitch adjacent to the basketball court. Sometimes these sessions went on late into the evenings and the school caretaker took home an extra pay-packet of tips each week for keeping the school gates open a little longer.

The enthusiasm amongst the parents for volleyball continued long after Mexico had been knocked out of the World Cup and became so intense that I persuaded Alejandra to allow me to organise a competition and to open it up to the town.

'Not only can we charge each team a nominal amount for entering the contest and these funds can be put towards purchasing new sports equipment but it will also be good publicity for the school,' I argued.

Eventually she agreed and I began planning the event in earnest. We got permission to use the local municipal courts at *Tierras Blancas* and within a week, 15 teams from around Valle had signed up to the tournament each paying an entry fee of 60 pesos. Local sports shops sponsored the contest donating volleyballs and nets, and shops and restaurants contributed a variety of different prizes from bottles of Champagne to complimentary meals. Hans Klost, himself a formidable player, offered to make the trophy and the result was a beautiful wooden sculpture of a figure reaching for a ball.

The day of the tournament arrived and over 300 people including players and spectators gathered at Tierras Blancas for what promised to be a very competitive event. Each team consisted of six players and had its own particular name. There were the *Pumas, Las Aztecas, Los Ganadores, Los Campeones* to name but a few. The School entered a team captained by the new caretaker, *Genaro* and he was joined by Mark, myself, *Clara*, the school secretary, Rocio and Sirani. For two weeks we practised for two hours after school until we had honed our skills and rehearsed our moves. My role was to receive the opponents' serve and volley it high into the air for either Mark or Genaro to smash over the net. Clara and Sirani, the best servers on the team, were expected to win as many points as they could when opposing teams conceded their serves. We felt ready. What we hadn't accounted for however, was the sheer professionalism and dedication of many of the other teams that had entered.

Sharon and Milli kept the scores and regularly updated the results on a white board by the side of the courts whilst Sal announced the order of play through a megaphone.

Although we played our hearts out and were supported by the pupils at the school who cheered and egged us on from the stand, we were eliminated in the first round by a team of 16 year old school girls who destroyed us in less than 20 minutes!

The competition was eventually won at eight o'clock in the evening after 10 hours of constant play, by Valle's motley crew of firemen who powered their way through to the final, narrowly beating Sergio's team in spite of his notorious moon balls!

CHAPTER 39

AMIGOS Y CONOCIDOS

We are going to the ambassador's house tomorrow. Dad is getting a medal from the queen. Mum says it's going to be an important ocasion. The ambassador has a glass eye. I hope I see the Rolls Royce and the body guards with their machine guns.

***

Walo *Miguel* became a good friend. His daughter, *Micaela* was one of my pupils and I soon learned that Walo (like me) was a keen tennis player.

Walo was second generation Mexican. His grandparents had emigrated from The Lebanon and he looked distinctly Middle Eastern. I pictured him on the set of 'Lawrence of Arabia' clad in a flowing, white kaftan and keffiyeh. For a Mexican he was very tall and at six foot six inches, towered over most Vallesanos.

Walo was one of Valle's entrepreneurs. He had been married to *Monica Patiño*, a celebrated chef and famous TV cook and for many years before they were separated they ran the *Taberna del Leon* near the lake, reputed to be one of the finest restaurants in Mexico.

When I met Walo he had his own pottery that produced bespoke dinner services and ornaments. He was also a bee keeper and sold his honey through exclusive Mexican delis and department stores such as Liverpool and Sanborns.

Walo lived in *Acatitlan*, an idylic spot some five miles out of Valle where a river ran gently through maize fields and potato drills and the houses were secluded with private gardens. It was an area favoured by writers and artists and the ocasional politician and millionaire. Walo's house was the epitome of good taste. Its walls were soft, warm, adobe brown and there were flowers and plants everywhere. Immaculate lawns dropped down to a brook at the end of the garden where there was the scent of mint and thyme.

The kitchen was fit for a restaurant. The centre piece was a huge stainless steel gas range. Built into a wall was a large wine rack where dusty bottles of vintage claret matured slowly. Shelves were stacked with jars of almonds and walnuts and herbs and spices: yellow saffron, curry powders, chillis of every kind and different coloured mustards. There were *Talavera* caserole dishes, frying pans of various sizes, dinner services and colourful Mexican glassware elegantly displayed on an antique dresser and in the rainy season, a fire glowed in the enormous hearth.

Once a week, I would drive up to Acatitlan to play tennis with Walo. He knew someone with a court and we would hop into his beach buggy and hurtle up the dirt track. We would play the best of three sets and although the games were always close; often ending in a tiebreak, I could rarely return his serve which came firing down at me with the speed of a bullet. Occasionally, I got my racket to it but by then Walo was looming at the net ready to smash the ball into oblivion!

Returning to the house there was always something delicious to eat: parma ham with a homegrown roquet salad, freshly made tamales, chicken mole, an avocado and prawn cocktail or a tortilla soup.

***

It was Walo's idea to bring a group of friends together to cook one night in his kitchen. Walo invited a number of people we knew in common. There was *Marga* and *Alejandro Calderon*, to whom I gave private English lessons. *Saulo* and his pretty wife *Pati* were there and a relatively new couple to Valle; the *Chavez-Peon*.

Saulo was someone I didn't have a lot of time for. He was a professional Mexican with his drooping bandido moustache and his penchant for sombreros and Stetsons. Saulo had to be the centre of attention, the life and soul of the party and was forever playing the role of the macho Mexican. When it became clear to everyone in Valle that he was besotted with Kristin Chavez-Peon, I lost all respect for him.

Kristin was Norwegian and was often compared to the actress Cameron Diaz. She was tall with blonde hair and quintessentially Scandinavian. Unlike most Mexican women, she was also gregarious and comfortable in the company of men which was often misinterpreted as flirtation by some of Valle's more traditional *hombres*, notably

Saulo. She had met her husband *Enrique* in Paris where they had both been studying French and they had two daughters in the school. Enrique was a glorified fishmonger from a well connected, wealthy family. He sold Norwegian and Canadian salmon to markets in the U.S and Europe.

Marga and Alejandro were among the first Mexicans I met when I arrived in Valle and they introduced me to many of their friends. Marga had an effusive personality and was an excellent networker organising parties and reunions to bring people together. She was also a very good volleyball player. Alejandro was an architect of Jewish extraction and looked distinctly Israeli. When I first met him I was reminded of Yitzhak Shamir.

That night, as lightning shattered the black sky and the last of the rains pounded down, we feasted on marinated tuna sashimi, beetroot soup, *bacalao* and the most heavenly pear and chocolate dessert. A woman with long grey hair read tea leaves and made outrageous predictions, and for half an hour Saulo was no longer the centre of attention. The year was drawing to a close and the Mayan calendar prophesised the end of civilization.

Over the weeks following the 'cookathon' at Walo's, Sharon and I saw a lot of the Calderons, Walo and the Chavez-Peons though we avoided Saulo like the plague. This was unfortunate only because Pati, his wife was a most warm and welcoming person.

***

We soon got to know other Mexican families. *Jose Luis* and *Laura Salamanca* were both heavily involved in the school as governors and shareholders. Jose Luis (another architect) enjoyed mountain biking and we cycled together to Ixtapan de la Sal and Real de Arriba. Laura had been a teacher at the school when it first opened and now ran an extracurricular ballet club. They both came to me for regular English lessons and we enjoyed their company.

We also got to know a number of expatriates who had settled in Valle. Peter MacGowan, with his clipped white moustache and BBC accent looked like an English army office. He was an Anglo-Argentine but aged 70 had only been to the U.K once when he was stationed in Harrogate at the end of the Second World War. He had retired to Mexico after working as an Engineer for Coleman in Buenos Aires. He had been briefly married to Jerit, also an expatriate from San Francisco. Jerit's parents were Italian immigrants and when their daughter was born they decided to call her after themselves. Her father was Jerry and her mother Rita – so they came up with the name Jerit! With her iron grey hair, beaky nose and glass eye, she was certainly someone you would look at twice, but she and Peter were like chalk and cheese. Jerit was bohemian and irascible. Peter was calm, composed – the perfect gentleman. People in Valle often wondered how they had ever got together in the first place. They too had a young son in La Escuela Valle de Bravo. Despite loathing each other, Jerit and Peter were neighbours and they went to great lengths to avoid one another. This could often be a logistical nightmare because both parents wished to be fully involved in the life of the school.

Jerit was a talented artist and the owner of Tash, one of Valle's many boutiques selling leather and suede goods and artists' materials. She lived in an organic house which she had hewn out of the hillside with her bare hands. The floors were baked adobe; the hat-stand, a lacquered branch in a plant pot. Seating and sofas were moulded into the walls using old railways sleepers which were then covered in plaster of Paris, painted and upholstered. Her beautiful handmade kitchen was made entirely from recycled materials which she had found in and around Valle.

Peter and I got on from the moment we met. His brother had been one of my father's clients at the Bank of London and South America in Buenos Aires and although Peter was many years my senior, we had a lot in common. He was an avid reader and liked to talk about literature and he too was an *aficionado* of all things Mexican. He would often invite me for a beer after school and we would sit on his terrace and talk about English football.

***

Sharon and I met Gill Cumiskey through Pua. They were both members of an international exchange programme and Pua had invited her to Mexico. Gill was tall and slim with long brown hair and blue eyes. She fell in love with Valle and soon got a job working as an administrator for a local hotel. Gill was different from other English people who ended up in Mexico. She was quirky and deeply involved in alternative medicines and therapies. With its curanderos and *temascals* she found a home in Mexico. We became good friends and saw her regularly. On rainy afternoons she would drop by for a cup of tea and would spend hours chatting and laughing with Sharon.

Gill's American boyfriend, Ray, came to visit and she brought him around to meet us. He was tall and dark and softy spoken and like me, loved the outdoors and was keen to explore the area. One Saturday I rented two kayaks from a contact I had met through the school and we paddled across the lake. It was nearing the end of the dry season and a strong southerly wind whipped up the waters into waves that crashed over our boats. The crossing and return took us eight hours as we dodged reckless jet skiers and high powered speed boats.

We met Texan Linda through the school where she was recruited as a part time science teacher. She was blonde, brassy and bubbly and spoke with a distinct southern drawl. Linda rented a house on a large hacienda on the outskirts of the town. Her landlord, *Josue Fernandez* was an eccentric Mexican in his late thirties. He was a passionate rider and owned several thoroughbred Arabs and Andalucian horses. The family hacienda, built in the late 19th century had a swimming pool, tennis courts, stables and gardens and even its own chapel and cantina. On first appearance Josue appeared to be your typical Mexican but Linda informed us that he enjoyed cross dressing and we once spotted him one night clad in a black skirt, black blouse and flowing black wig.

Linda had spent a year living in *Puerto Angel* on Mexico's Pacific coast. She told us the story of how an arrogant young American disappeared suddenly one night after offending some locals.

'I can't remember the guy's name,' she said, 'but he was one of those jerks that give us gringos down here a real bad reputation. He worked in a surfing shop and liked to hang out in all the bars and thought he was a hit with the girls. One night he seduced the young daughter of a local politician and got her pregnant. She was only 17. When the family found out, the brothers invited him out for a night on the town, got him drunk and then took him out to sea on their *lancha* and fed him to the sharks.'

***

Among the parents at the school were a number of celebrated Mexicans. *Carlos Carsolio* moved to Valle and put his two children into the primary. Carlos was Mexico's top mountaineer and was renown within the international climbing fraternity as the youngest alpinist to have climbed the 14 highest peaks on earth including Everest, K2 and Kachenjunga. He was dark with a friendly open face and built like a rugby prop but in spite of his reputation was extremely modest and a great supporter of the school. His former wife, *Elsa Avila* was also a mountaineer of international repute and the first woman in Latin America to reach the summit of Everest.

Miguel Rodriguez was a world champion paraglider pilot and owned a flying school in Valle. Due to its geographical position between the volcanic ridge of the Nevado de Toluca and tierra caliente to the south, Valle provided some of the best flying conditions in the world with thermal air currents rising from the coast. Local hills were popular launch pads for both national and international pilots.

One weekend an American flyer from Seattle invited me to fly tandem with him. We drove up to *El Peñon* (a huge sugar loaf hill above Zacazonapan) with a group from Canada and spent an hour paragliding over Valle. The views were spectacular. I spotted the school and Acatitlan far below and to the north the towns of Amanalco and Donata Guerra. Harnessing one of nature's most powerful forces was an incredible feeling.

Luis Lopez Loza was one of Mexico's most famous contemporary artists and he chose to base himself in Valle when he was not travelling and exhibiting in the States and Europe. Knowing Sharon was a keen artist he invited her to his weekly life classes which he held in his spacious house on the outskirts of Ottumba. Luis was a gentle, mild mannered man and his daughter had been a pupil at the school. He had known many of Mexico's acclaimed artists including *Frida Kahlo, David Siqueiros* and *Rufino Tamayo*.

CHAPTER 40

PERROS SALVAJES

We are in Valle with the Russells who have come out from England. Dad says he has brought us a surprise. It's under a large blanket in the dining room. Jason and I are sure it's a motorbike. Later dad reveals what it is. It's a Piñata. Jason and I are bitterly disappointed but we try not to show it.

***

Rancho *Feshi* was situated some 10 miles out of Valle near the town of Amanalco. It specialised in trout (which were farmed on the premises), its flat oven baked breads and its micheladas. There was nothing fancy about Rancho Feshi – diners shared tables sitting on long benches in the large hall and the floors were covered in sawdust. But the food was delicious and well worth the journey and lack of sophistication.

Sharon was down for the last weekend of term and I would not be seeing her for several weeks as Mark and I were planning on cycling to Guatemala. Nancy and Robert had told us about Rancho Feshi so we decided to drive out there for lunch. I had been back in Mexico almost a year and the rainy season was once again upon us. As we drove out of Valle through wooded hills towards the village of Amanalco, I recalled the journey that had brought me back to Mexico. Twelve months before I had been a struggling freelance journalist in London paying an exhorbitent rent for a room in a shared house. Mexico then, was only a childhood memory. I had been offered a job in Oman as editor of a travel magazine but had turned it down. Deserts were not really my thing, though I knew people who had explored the Empty Quarter and they had talked about its lonely beauty. I had considered other jobs too including one as a guide in Alaska's Mount Elias National Park but just getting there was going to cost a small fortune. Destiny, I believed had beckoned me back to Mexico!

A crude wooden sign on the side of the road just before the town directed us off onto a dirt track that led to the roadhouse. With stomachs already rumbling with hunger, we pushed open the swinging doors and were met by a merry faced Otomi woman in an apron. '*Señores*,' she said apologetically, 'We are having problems lighting the ovens – food will not be ready for another half an hour!'

Although the skies were leaden, it was not raining, so we decided to go for a short walk to whet our appetites further. We took a path that meandered by the trout ponds up into the woods and were soon looking down on the ranch below us where two mangy mongrels barked at us from a distance. It wasn't long before other dogs trotted out from behind some huts and began barking too and soon we counted a pack of 8 hounds of various shapes and sizes. We continued climbing for a further five minutes but stopped when we heard the large alpha male coming up behind us growling. Others dogs joined him, snapping and within seconds the pack had surrounded us and several of the dogs were snarling and baring their teeth. Sharon gripped my hand tightly and her knuckles went white.

'I don't like this at all,' she said putting on a brave face.

I slowly bent down and picked up a stick and began waving it at the dogs but this only provoked them even more and they inched forward ready to attack.

'This may sound stupid,' said Sharon, 'but I think we should sit down, that way we won't seem like a threat to them.'

We slowly sat down on a pile of damp pine needles and tried to ignore the dogs. Seconds passed like minutes and I feared that if the pack attacked us now we had little chance of escaping a severe mauling. Neither of us spoke. And then the large male that resembled a German shepherd, suddenly stopped snarling and began whimpering. He lowered his head, his ears pricked up and after sniffing around us he began to lick our faces. The other dogs soon lost interest and wandered off but the German shepherd lay down next to us panting. We waited several minutes, our hearts still pounding, before getting up and slowly retracing our steps down to the ranch. By the time we reached the dining room there wasn't a dog in sight. When the Otomi woman came to take our order we enquired about the dogs.

'They are wild,' she said. 'They roam these hills looking for food. Every now and again the pest control people round them up and shoot them but more always come. You need to be careful,' she warned us. 'Some of them probably carry rabies.'

***

When we were living in Mexico in the 1970's a friend of my brother's was bitten by a rabid dog. Richard, then aged only nine, had to have a course of 12 very painful injections in his stomach. People in Mexico were rightly terrified of the disease, since it often proved fatal, especially in rural areas which were often miles from medical services. I remember being told as a child that rabies caused insanity, hypersalivation and hydrophobia. I pictured people foaming at the mouth fearful of water. It was the subject of childhood nightmares. In those days many Mexicans believed that you had to catch a rabid dog and decapitate it or its victim wouldn't survive. I feared that Pancho, our dog, who had a propensity to find his way out of the garden and roam the streets, would catch rabies and that we would find his head or decapitated corpse on scrub land nearby but fortunately we never did.

When he did finally disappear, shortly before we left Mexico, we spent weeks walking the streets posting pictures and notices on lampposts and through neighbours' doors. 'Had anyone seen a black and white spotted dog that was part Labrador part Dalmatian and went by the name of Pancho?' My parents were inundated with replies but none of them led to his discovery or shed any light on what had become of him. Several neighbours responded telling us that Pancho visited them daily often spending hours playing in their gardens or sitting on their kitchen floors. One woman was distraught. 'Pancho,' she wrote, 'would often lie on the bed with me whilst I was reading in the afternoon!' We had to laugh. We knew he had an insatiable desire to roam, but we never knew that he had led such a secret life!

CHAPTER 41
A CHIAPAS

We are leaving Mexico. Dad has been posted to Venezuela. There's lots of oil there and jungle. Adela will join us in two months time. I'll miss Alberto and Juventino.

***

The academic year ended on the 18th of July and two days later Mark and I set off on our two week bike ride to explore southern Mexico. Our plan was to cycle from *Puebla* to the Guatemalan border via the city of Oaxaca, the *Tehuantepec* Isthmus and the state of Chiapas.

Our first stop was *Tehuacan*, 70 miles south of Puebla. We arrived in its lively tree lined square late in the afternoon after a six hour bike ride along a dead straight road, aided by a southerly wind.

Tehuacan was a neat little town, known throughout Mexico for its mineral water. We found accommodation in the once grand Hotel Madrid overlooking the parish church with its brightly coloured tiled dome. Our rooms smelt faintly damp but we had our own bathroom, there was plenty of hot water and the beds were soft and springy.

With our departure from Tehuacan along the old Oaxaca road, we left behind the heavy traffic as we cycled in the early morning light through small dusty villages and maize fields. The day's climb began just outside the village of *Teotitlan* where we stopped at a trucker's diner for a breakfast of ham, eggs and tortillas. The climb, when it came was relentless and we made a snail's progress up a series of tight switchbacks in the midday sun. Around each bend we hoped to see the road begin to descend but the summit continued to elude us. Little grew in these hot brown hills but cacti and thorns. We soon ran out of water and took longer over our rest stops, sitting on the rocky edge of the dusty road, sweat pouring down our faces. Eventually at four in the afternoon we reached the top of a high pass and looked down on a fertile, green valley with a large, muddy river flowing through it.

The previous day, Mark had cycled with his bike seat too low resulting in a strained knee tendon which was now giving him considerable pain. So it was with relief that we cycled into the village of *Cuicatllan,* hidden among trees and sugar cane fields below some crumbly, red cliffs.

We found a posada a five minute walk away from the Zocalo. A grumpy indigena with rotten teeth and dermatitis showed us to our room and then promptly pulled up a chair outside and watched us unpack our bikes.

Our cell had no window, just a sky light set high in one wall with a grill across it. I wondered if it had been a prison since there were several large iron rings in the wall and the building was built like a fortress.

After a cold shower in the communal bath-house, we went out to explore the village. Opposite the inn was a shop selling herbal medicines and potions. Large jars stuffed with different coloured leaves and twigs and one containing what looked like chicken legs, lined the shelves. The shop smelt of arnica and garlic. The village square was empty except for a few old men sitting silently on benches. We passed the open doors of a cantina and spotted a pool table. On average, Mark and I had played pool three times a week back in Valle, but whilst Mark's game had greatly improved, mine seem to deteriorate, but the competition was always heated and accompanied by a great deal of cursing as we potted balls, missed or conceded penalty shots.

Cuicatllan's cantina was to be the venue for several more frames of our ongoing feud. As we stepped in, all eyes turned on us. There was a pool table free and we asked if we could play. As we racked up the balls and picked our cues, everyone gathered around and a group of passing children filled the doorway to watch the gringos. Our cantina audience was a motley group of fat old men and thin youths swigging bottles of Corona beer.

I won the first two frames and was beginning to get cocky. Then in the third, Mark potted the black with a shot that rebounded off the cushion and he was back in the game. With growing excitement and exclamations from the crowd, Mark went on to win the next three frames.

We stayed in Cuicatllan for two nights for Mark to rest his knee. Apart from games of pool we spent the days taking refuge from the sapping heat, reading and eating in a wonderful little restaurant that served pizzas with thick Oaxaca cheese and mushrooms.

We left Cuicatllan on our fourth day out from Puebla on a road that snaked higher and higher into the Oaxacan sierra. There was no traffic on this dirt track and we enjoyed the solitude of the hills making frequent stops to admire the scenery and to take photographs. These remote mountains were home to Zapotec indigenas. They spoke in lilting, sing-song tones and made meagre livings off the harsh terrain, terracing the hillsides to grow maize and graze herds of goat.

Our destination was the pre-Colombian city of Oaxaca lying in a vast valley and after a long day in the saddle we eventually arrived at five o'clock in its elegant square. We quickly discovered that the Zocalo was the geographical and social epicentre of the city where the majority of the tourists were congregated, seated at tables under the arcades drinking coffee and beers and watching the world go by. Throughout the afternoon and evening, as we sat over our micheladas, a small army of buskers, clowns, basket makers, rug pedlars, rebozos weavers and souvenir hawkers pursued their trades in the shade of the colonnades. In the square, children roller skated, travellers pored over maps and guidebooks and balloon and candyfloss vendors lingered around the restaurants.

Our *pension* was sandwiched between two chocolate factories, from which a delicious smell of cinnamon and cocoa wafted down the street. The neighbourhood was buzzing with activity around Oaxaca's huge indoor market. It was also the red light district and at dusk, heavily made up women in stilettos and tight miniskirts gathered in doorways chatting and waiting, their cigarettes glowing like fire flies in the night.

We stayed three nights in Oaxaca. I spent a whole day walking around the city using the zocalo as my central reference point. Despite its antiquity, the layout of the city seemed distinctly modern with parallel streets running in all directions making exploration relaxingly easy. After breakfast, I walked north along *Macedonio Alcala* to the church of *Santo Domingo*. In the early morning light, the sandy coloured stone of the *ayuntamiento* and other municipal buildings looked particularly warm. But there were also bolder colours: pink and pastel coloured houses with avocado, terracotta and ochre doors and shops selling local crafts: rugs, carpets, jewellery and hammocks; brightly coloured woven shirts, wall hangings and ceramics.

Santo Domingo church at the top of the street was reputed to be one of the most beautiful examples of Baroque architecture in the Americas. It was built like a castle with walls eight feet thick and had withstood earthquakes, revolution and civil war.

Oaxaca is renowned gastronomically for its tamales and moles. Tamales (steamed corn dumplings served in banana leaves and stuffed with a variety of vegetables, meat and sauces) are amongst the oldest Mexican dishes and were served at Aztec banquets. In Oaxaca, there were streets of shops and restaurants that specialised in them. On our second day in the city we ventured into the food market. Inside, dozens of food stalls with their own tables and benches vied for customers.

'*Tenemos tamales, tortas, y comida corrida – pasen le,* 'shouted cooks from every corner and alcove.

We stopped at a stall where a huge bosomed woman was stirring a cauldron of soup. We ordered chicken mole with rice and tortillas and cold beers.

***

Mole – pronounced 'molay' (derived from the *Nahautl* word *moli,* meaning sauce or concoction) is another Mexican speciality of which *Oaxacans* are particularly proud. There were many versions of mole and each barrio in Oaxaca claimed to have the most delicious. English cookbooks often translate mole as 'turkey in chocolate sauce,' a misnomer since mole contains only about an ounce of chocolate which is added as a sweetener. Its rich, dark colour is obtained from the dried chillies used in its preparation.

Oaxaca's market was a fascinating place to 'people watch.' There were solo guitarists, marimba bands and mariachis serenading and even a young boy aged about ten who sang old Mexican ballads for 15 pesos. Apart from the cooking and eating there was a constant flow of street vendors: boys selling pirate cassettes, old men carrying strings of leather sandals, young girls selling woven bracelets and silver jewellery. There were beggars sitting on the floor, children playing and running about in bare feet and old women selling buckets of blackberries and grasshoppers, another Mexican delicacy. Eating in the market was a vision of what life in Europe might have been like in the Middle Ages – a constant pageant of colour, odours, noise and vibrant activity.

***

On leaving Oaxaca to the southeast we set our sights on the village of *Camaron* on the banks of the *Rio Grande*, 56 miles away. Getting there involved hours of steep climbing before we finally descended down an exhilarating 13 miles of tight hairpin bends. In the early evening we entered a dark canyon carved out by the river. Here the road was so steep we topped speeds of 44 miles an hour. Great black buzzards hovered overhead and the roar of the wind and the river was deafening.

Camaron was just a collection of corrugated iron shacks and a trucker's stop. For a few pesos we were served a delicious meal of vegetable soup, steak, rice and fried potatoes. After supper we spent the evening poring over our newly acquired set of topographical maps which we had bought from the regional offices of the National Geographical Institute in Oaxaca. They were an invaluable resource, for at scale of 1:25,000 they detailed every river and town, but more importantly every climb and every descent. At eight o'clock, after a freezing cold shower, we doused ourselves in mosquito repellent and went to bed.

We knew that our last day in the Oaxacan Sierra, as we dropped down to the coast would be a long one, so we were up and on the road at five o'clock. A low, damp mountain mist hung over Camaron and the tropical hills surrounding it. We set off in a light, refreshing drizzle and climbed steadily higher through lush vegetation. By seven o'clock the rain had ceased and the early morning sun filtered through the fog in spectacular rainbows. Miles and miles of tropical hills rolled away to the south. From the dense canopy of trees and wayside undergrowth came a cacophony of insect and birdsong.

From time to time we stopped to check our position on the map. Various villages lay in our path before the descent to the coast: *La Capilla, La Navaja, La Peña Gorda* and last of all – the weather station at *La Reforma*.

A further hour and a half of climbing brought us to the sierra's summit and the start of our rapid descent. After five minutes of freewheeling, I stopped to adjust my bike seat and told Mark that I would catch up with him. The route down the mountain was clear for miles so I was confident that I could keep him in sight, but when I resumed cycling, he was nowhere to be seen. As I sped down the hillside, I passed a truck parked by the side of the road and saw a man wheeling a black bike into some bushes. It looked suspiciously like Mark's. Several worrying thoughts passed through my mind. Before we had set out we had heard the usual horror stories about travelling in rural Mexico. But none of these had put us off before. Now, however the words of one particular friend came into my mind:

'It's extremely dangerous,' *Fernando* had warned. 'If you are assaulted or run over by a car, there will be no one to help you. Most drivers in Mexico are not insured. If you are hit by a car, the driver will probably make sure that you are dead and hide the evidence!'

As I scanned the dry canyons and the road below me for signs of Mark through my binoculars, Fernando's sober words came to mind. Perhaps the truck back there had hit Mark and the driver had taken the bike and hidden his body?

After several anxious miles of cycling, however I spotted Mark ahead of me and with great relief found him resting on a bridge, a wet handkerchief over his face.

'I thought you were close behind me,' he said, smiling.

'I thought you were dead,' I replied and explained why.

'You wouldn't have seen me because I took my bike down to the river when I went to refill my water bottles.'

***

After another hour of reckless descent we found ourselves in the hot, sticky Isthmus of *Tehuantepec*, Mexico's narrowest stretch of land between the Pacific and the Atlantic Ocean. We were now out of the mountains and the sea, although we could not not see it, was only 10 miles away. Mirages hovered over the horizon and two large iguanas crossed the road lethargically in front of us. The heat was almost unbearable and within minutes our shirts were dripping with sweat and melting sun tan lotion was pouring down our faces. In spite of the heat, we made good progress along a road as flat as a pancake. Thirty miles from Tehuantepec, we stopped for lunch and a short rest under the shade of a palapa that served swordfish soup and ice cold beers.

Tehuantepec was situated among low brown hills on the wide bend of a muddy river. Although plagued by burning winds and sandstorms the town was nevertheless attractive and colourful and we felt more than relieved when we chained up our bikes in the square and fell into some comfortable chairs outside a local bar.

We spent the night in the Hotel Oasis behind the square after a supper of chicken in garlic with rice. The town was so small that a walk of five blocks in any direction would take you into the countryside. Despite this, or perhaps because Tehuantapec was concentrated into such a small area, it was hellishly noisy at night with a constant din of motorcycles, buses and taxis passing by.

The following day was to be the most perilous of the trip. As we cycled south, a vicious side wind whipped across the isthmus from east to west and we were constantly being blown into heavy traffic, most of it comprised of container lorries bound for Guatemala. Three times we were driven off the road. On one occasion I was shunted down a steep embankment on the edge of a swamp and went over my handlebars into thick elephant grass. Every so often a lorry would come so close we had to push ourselves away to avoid being sucked under the wheels. For Mark, the ordeal was agony. His knee, which had given him problems at the beginning of the ride, had swollen up and he was in great pain. Soon, without realising it, I was miles ahead of him, so much was I trying to concentrate on steering a straight course as the wind battered me from one side and the convoy of trucks threatened to plough me down from the other. After three hours of severe discomfort, Mark had to dismount and walk his bike. When we finally met up in the village of *Ventosa* 50 miles out of Tehuantepec, his knee had seized up and he could no longer bend it. There was only one thing to do: rest it up for the remainder of the day. In the pouring rain the village of *Tatantepec*, 10 miles further down the road, looked a grim place to spend a wet afternoon. The road was lined with the rusting remains of trucks and old buses and the place smelt of oil and rotting rubbish. But our one night stop there turned out to be a pleasant surprise at the end of a miserable day.

Off the road and obscured by a wall covered in a rampant bougainvillea, was a small casa de huesepedes with a bar restaurant and two spotlessly clean rooms with en-suite bathrooms and hot running water. The only incident that marred our stay was when the fan, suspended from the ceiling, collided with the light bulb and I was showered in glass!

Our evening meal of bean soup and coriander, tortillas and chicken washed down with several bottles of Corona beer was the perfect end to a difficult day and made our ordeal on the road seem a worthwhile struggle.

***

We never made it to the Guatemalan border. The swelling around Mark's knee had worsened over night and had spread down his leg like a puffy red blister. He was incapable of cycling more than a few miles and the border was still a two day ride away over mountainous terrain. We decided to call it a day. Instead we would cycle as far as Chiapas, 20 miles away where we would catch a bus to Tuxla Gutierrez, the state capital.

We headed for *Ariaga*, the first town over the state border. We cycled along a disused pot holed road where the season's rain had collected in deep muddy pools. Our only companions on the road were a few emaciated donkeys and the occasional bullock cart driven by dark skinny youths.

Reaching journey's end was a big anticlimax. There was nothing to do or see in Ariaga. The dusty town was built up around its bus terminal which looked incongruously clean and modern with its plate glass windows, shiny marble floor, cafe and bookshop. I wondered why there was a need for such a sophisticated bus station in this shabby town. Most rural terminals in Mexico were little more than corrugated shacks smelling of urine, but a closer look at the destinations board hanging over the ticket booths provided me with the answer. Ariaga served as a junction for services between Guatemala and the Gulf of Mexico, Tehuantepec and the rest of Chiapas.

We checked the timetable and found that there was a bus bound for Tuxla in 40 minutes. After buying tickets we sat down in the cafe for a greasy breakfast of fried eggs, re-fried beans and bacon to reflect on our two week journey. As we sat in our filthy clothes and contemplated our long journey back to Valle, I thought of Robert Louis Stephenson. 'To travel hopefully is a better thing than to arrive, and the true success is to labour.'[2*]

***

It was pouring with rain when I arrived back in Valle late at night after an exhausting 18 hour bus journey from Chiapas. By the time I reached my front gate, Culebra was a muddy stream and the town was utterly silent save for a dog barking in the distance.

Once inside, I lit a candle and shedding my sodden clothes, I had a hot shower. No one had been in the house for two weeks. The storm had cut off the electricity and the house was full of cobwebs. I propped my pillows up and lay on the bed to watch the storm outside through the large windows. For a moment I felt like a stranger again in the house. I could smell the damp again and the rain outside. I closed my eyes and listened to the rumbling of thunder, the glass shaking in the windowframe and the pitter-patter of the rain on my roof. More dogs began barking in the valley and a mosquito droned somewhere in the room. And then I fell asleep.

∽

EPILOGUE

CRUSANDO MEXICO

'Memory is satisfied desire' – **Carlos Fuentes**

***

The bus from Veracruz to *Alvarado* rattled south along a rutted potholed road. Torrential rain lashed against the cracked window panes and pelted the roof of the bus like ballbearings. Simon and I had arrived in Mexico City early that morning on a trans Atlantic flight from London. Stowed underneath the rusting bus were two mountain bikes – our transport for the next three weeks as we attempted to cycle across the Republic from the Atlantic to the Pacific over the Sierra Madre Mountains. This was Simon's first visit to Mexico. He sat with his face glued to the filthy window, taking in the passing sights: rain drenched villages, fields of sugar cane, bullock drawn carts moving slowly along country lanes, ancient cars, indigenas carrying machetes and women wheeling barrows of fruit to market.

After a two hour bus journey from the port city of Veracruz we arrived in sleepy Alvarado where we found lodgings in the town's dilapidated posada. Our room was dark and dank, and brown water dripped from the taps in the bathroom but it was just a place to lay our heads for a night or two as we prepared for the road.

***

Founded in 1518, by the Spanish adventurer, Pedro Alvarado, the town quickly became a thriving port in the 16th century, exporting sugar and coffee to the West Indies and other Spanish Colonies. Today, Alvarado is a quiet fishing village on the Gulf of Mexico bordered by the *Papaloapan River* which meanders through mangroves and flamingo flats. It's a town ravaged by hurricanes, sapping humidity and mosquitoes but nonetheless it has an offbeat charm. It's not on the tourist trail and few have reason to visit it but the people were welcoming and friendly and there's not a better fish soup to be had anywhere else in Mexico!

***

I met Simon working as a teacher in a school in Leeds in 2005. He was tall and slim and had an uncanny resemblance to a young Clint Eastwood. Knowing that he enjoyed the 'Big Outdoors' I approached him half way through the term and suggested doing a charity mountain bike ride to raise funds for a local hospice.

'Sounds good to me,' was his response, 'where were you thinking of going?'

I told him that it had been years since Sharon and I had left Mexico after the birth of our first son and that I was itching to get back. I was planning on cycling across the country from east to west via the City of Oaxaca. We would try to avoid metalled roads as much as possible and cycle between remote mountain villages. The whole trip would last about three weeks.

Simon's reaction was instantly enthusiastic.

'Fantastic; so long as we can eat plenty of chillies and drink lots of Tequila – I'm game!'

***

From Alvarado we cycled west through swamps and waterlogged fields of sugar cane. Vultures flew overhead and the oven hot wind carried with it the stench of carrion. Nothing eased the monotony of the road, the haze of mosquitoes or the heat until we arrived in colourful *Tlacocalpan* situated on the bend of a river. Here, there was a cobbled plaza with statues and colonades and restaurants serving breakfast and fresh fruit juices. The town was unmistakably tropical. There were palm trees and the buildings were an eclectic mix of orches, oranges, reds and pinks. By comparison with other towns in the state of Veracruz, it was spotlessly clean with bougainvillea running riot over ancient dry stone walls

It was eight o'clock in the morning and we had already been cycling for two hours. We slumped into wicker chairs in the zocalo and ordered huevos rancheros and a jug of orange and pineapple juice. After a long term with little time for exercise

Simon and I were desperately unfit and unprepared for the exhausting heat and humidity.

A day later we found ourselves in seedy *Papaloapan* where we were forced to stop for two nights. Simon had a severe case of Moctezuma's revenge and had collapsed from dehydration despite drinking copious amounts of bottled water and Dioralyte. While he lay in bed sleeping and sweating deliriously, I wandered the grubby streets taking photographs and sitting in bars reading. By the end of our second day in the town, with Simon's condition showing no signs of improvement, I was worried that he might have to be hospitalised and that would be the end of our expedition. But overnight he recovered and I awoke to find him dressed and oiling his bike:

'Rise and shine mate,' he said cheerfully. 'We've got some serious catching up to do!'

***

Papaloapan at six o'clock in the morning was silent save for the *cicadas* and a dog barking somewhere in the distance. We cycled south along the main street and a mine field of rain filled potholes and crossed the river. Just past the village, the track rose dramatically, snaking its way through the grey dawn into thick jungle and cloud forest. From around a bend in the dirt road, we could hear a truck approaching and then we were momentarily blinded by its headlights as it came trundling down the hill towards us. It stopped abruptly and the driver leant out of the window.

'Don't go any further,' he warned ominously. 'Turn back to the village, there's a puma prowling around the edge of the track.'

I looked around at Simon. 'He's pulling a fast one. He thinks we are a couple of stupid gringos!'

We thanked the driver for his concern and cycled on. Turning back was not an option. Ahead of us was a monumental climb of 9,000 feet to the hamlet of *El Machin* which we had to reach to stay on schedule. Mounting our bikes we crept on and up the endless switchbacks with the thought that a mountain lion might indeed be stalking us. And then we saw her – sleek and iron grey against the pink dawn, six feet in length, ears erect with paws the size of dinner plates. She was about the height of a Great Dane. She looked at us for a moment and then was gone into the density of the forest. That's when our hearts began pounding and the adrenalin began to pump. We pedalled liked madmen, past the point where the puma had slunk off into the jungle, desperate to get as much distance from us and the big cat as possible.

***

Six hours later, and slimy with sweat we reached the hamlet of El Machin, a few miles below *La Peña Blanca* where we pulled up outside a shabby cantina. A police truck was parked in the dust. We pushed open the swinging doors and ordered cups of café de olla. The policemen briefly looked up at us before returning to their game of cards, their machine guns and rifles propped up against the wall. A few moments later a fat *sargento* pulled a revolver from its holster and slapped it on the table. 'Now let's see who the real men are,' I overheard him say in Spanish. 'Let's play a little roulette like the *bandidos* did in the old days.' His companions looked at him silently, beads of sweat appearing on their brows. '*Pepe*,' he said, addressing a young man with a wispy moustache and bad teeth, 'you're the youngest – you go first!' There was silence for a minute and then Pepe nervously picked up the gun, rammed it into his mouth and pulled the trigger. Simon and I flinched and looked away. And then we heard *Pepe* drop the gun on the table and run outside where he was violently sick. His colleagues sniggered as he returned, ashen faced, wiping his mouth with the back of his hand. The barmaid made herself scarce and we found ourselves the only witnesses to this terrifying game. The sargento then took up the gun. 'To show you guys that I am not a pussy I'll go next,' he boasted and raised the revolver slowly to his temple. He was about to pull the trigger when the crackly sound of a voice was heard over his radio. He lowered the gun and replaced it in its holster before taking the call. 'They want us over in *Chilutla* to deal with some *narcos*,' he told his colleagues. They drained their cups of coffee, picked up their weapons and were gone.

***

We camped that night under a lone acacia tree on a high plateau surrounded by a herd of big horned cattle grazing on the upland pastures. A bank of thick white cloud rose slowly from the jungle below, backed by an orange sky. It was tempting to think that the route to the Pacific coast would be all downhill from here, but the Sierra Madre was interlaced with several deep valleys and ravines all of which we had to negotiate.

Seventy miles from Oaxaca as we were descending a steep ravine, Simon swerved unexpectedly in front of me as his luggage rack shifted and then flew off shedding its load over the side of the canyon. The sudden loss of weight at the back of his bike combined with the speed he as travelling sent Simon skidding across the track and he ended up in a tangled heap by the trailside. Fortunately he suffered only minor cuts and abrasions. He was far more concerned about his equipment that now lay dispersed among bushes down the steep sides of the cliff. Leaving our bikes we crept down the precarious scree that dropped 1000 feet down to the river. Simon spotted his orange sleeping bag in a thicket and then other items; a sleeping mat, parts of the tent he'd been carrying and a first aid kit strewn across the boulder field. After retrieving them, we crept back up the slope fearing our movement would cause a landslide and we we'd be swept into the abyss. The rack was twisted and bent so we had to improvise using thin nylon ties to re-attach it to the bike. It rattled and moved from side to side and looked at any moment as if it would fly off the bike again but we made it down into the Valley of Oaxaca without further incident and joined the metalled road leading to the city's outskirts.

After a day and a half of rest and recreation in Oaxaca and the relative luxury of a hotel room, air conditioning and power showers, we hit the road again. Over two days we cycled liked demons covering 161 miles, fit after our mountain marathon. Now we faced the sparsely populated *Sierra Madre Occidental*, a series of high mountains covered in pine forest. On our second day out of Oaxaca we were caught in a tropical downpour briefly heralded by a flash of lightning. Within seconds our clothes were wringing wet but we had little choice but to continue cycling. The terrain was too steep to pitch our tent and we were battling against time. A further two hours of cycling brought us to the chilly summit and the miracle of a roadside shack selling cups of cafe de olla. Simon and I set up camp under the shelter of a corrugated iron corral where we lit a fire and attempted to dry off.

Two days later we found ourselves in the jungle again – this time in the small town of *San Gabriel de Mixtepec*. We lodged in the town's *casa de huespedes* where for the equivalent of five pounds we had a room with two filthy mattresses and geckos climbing on the walls. Journey's end was so tantalisingly close we could almost smell the sea. A dawn rise and a determination to be on the beach by ten o'clock spurred us on and up the last of the hills and the final 30 miles to the coast. The heat and humidity were so intense that after only half an hour's cycling our shirts were wet through with sweat. And then, as if no time at all had passed, we had reached the outskirts of Puerto Escondido and began following signs for *La Playa*. Fishermen, hauling long boats onto the beach fresh from their catches glanced up momentarily from folding their nets as we attempted to cycle across the sand and down to the sea. I fell over the handlebars and Simon slid gracefully sideways off his bike but we made it into the water: we had cycled across Mexico coast to coast.

- El Fin –

GLOSSARY

Chapter 1

Agua	water
Calle	street/road
Culebra	snake/serpent
Doña	the female of Don – an honorific title
Jacaranda	a subtropical tree native to C. America and S. America
Llegada	arrival
Mazahua	indigenous people inhabiting the State of Mexico
Pagaza	Mexican bishop and poet c 1839
Paleta	a fresh fruit ice lolly
Paseo	stroll
Peso	the Mexican currency
Pino	pine
Poncho	a woven shawl worn as a waterproof
Rebozo	a woven Mexican shawl

San	saint
Santa Maria	Saint Mary – a neighbourhood of Valle
Vendo leña	wood for sale
Veracruz	a state and sea port on the Gulf of Mexico
Náhuatl	the native language of the Aztecs
Zocalo	the Náhuatl word for a town square

Chapter 2

Antiguo	old/ancient
Avenida	avenue
Bienvenidos	welcome
Chicle	chewing gum
Jalapeño	pertaining to Jalapa
Madre	mother
Occidental	west/western
Pueblo	town
Sierra	mountain range
Toluca	capital city of the State of Mexico
Valle por Monumento	to Valle via Monumento

GLOSSARY

Xinantecatl — the Náhuatl name for Mexico's 4th highest volcano

Chapter 3

Benito Juarez — Zapotec president who served from 1858-1961

Enchiladas — a corn tortilla filled with chicken, cream and chilli and baked in the oven

Federales — federal police

Gringo — a slang term to denote foreigners

Indigena — a native/native people of Mexico

Marchante — a market stall holder/street seller

Maricon — a slang/derogatory term for a homosexual

Mercado — market

Morelos — Mexican Revolutionary/name of a Mexican state

Piñata — clay effigy, covered in colourful strips of paper and filled with sweets

Ranchito — a small holding/farm

Señor — Sir/Mr

Chapter 4

Escuela	school
Guerro	slang term for blonde
Hola	hello
Machete	a long cleaver-like cutting tool
Mestizo	a colonial Spanish term for a person of mixed blood
Plutarco Calles	Mexican general and politician 1877-1945
Sombrero	broad brimmed straw hat
Vallesano	a native of Valle

Chapter 5

Charro	a traditional Mexican cowboy
Chicharon	pork crackling
Grito	shout/scream; associated with the Independence fiesta
Mariachi	travelling musicians originally from Jalisco
Pozole	a pre-Colombian soup traditionally prepared at fiestas
Viva Mexico	long live Mexico

GLOSSARY

Chapter 7

Cine — cinema
La Peña — a prominent peak in the vicinity of Valle

Chapter 8

Lagartija — lizard
La Vista — view

Chapter 9

Cerro Gordo — a prominent hill in the vicinity of Valle
Corona — crown/ the trademark of a Mexican beer
El Pinal — a mountain hamlet in the vicinity of Valle
La vela de la novia — (the bride's veil) a waterfall & popular sight in Valle
Muy buena onda — a 'good egg'/slang for an amiable person
Tertulia — a social gathering

Chapter 10

La matanza   massacre

Chapter 11

Las lluvias   the rains/the rainy season
Peon   a labourer

Chapter 12

Alcazar   castle
Almuerzo   a light lunch
Bocadillo   a sándwich
Chulito   a term of endearment/ cute, cutie

Chapter 13

Chiapas   Mexico's southern most state bordering Guatemala
Gabriel Garcia Marquez   Colombian novelist born in 1927
Pampa   grasslands
Vagabundo   tramp/traveller

GLOSSARY

Yucatan a state of Mexico on the Yucatan Peninsular
Zihuatanejo fishing village on the Pacific coast of Mexico

Chapter 14

Barrio neighbourhood
Cafe de olla coffee sweetened with spices
Callejon an alleyway
Comida
corrida a three course set menu
El Dorado fabled lost city of Gold
Frijoles beans
La comida meal
Liquadora blender/liquidiser
Monjas nuns
Putitas derogatory term for prostitutes
Quesadillas a snack made from tortillas and melted cheese
Tacos a corn tortilla wrapped around a filling
Taqueria taco stall

Chapter 15

Cantina Mexican bar

Judiciales	plain clothed detectives/police
Pendejo	slang for 'ass hole'/ idiot
Viaducto	viaduct/name of a road in Mexico City

Chapter 16

Atole	a hot drink made from cornflour
Dia de los muertos	the Day of The Dead
Margaritas	a Tequila based cocktail

Chapter 17

Cajetas	sweet confectionary made from goats' milk
El niño	boy/a climate pattern particular to the Gulf of Mexico
Maguey	a type of cacti
Mariposas	butterflies
Otomi	an indigenous people of Mexico
Oyamel	a fir tree native to the Sierra Madre, Mexico
Refresco	a sweet carbonated drink
Relampago	lightning

GLOSSARY

Chapter 18

Andale guerro	good luck
Conejo	rabbit
Hacia las montañas	into the mountains
Los Borrachos	the drunkards/title of a painting by Velazquez
Terrazeria	dirt track/road

Chapter 19

Campamento	camp
Chorizo	cured pork sausage
Pan dulce	sweet pastries

Chapter 20

Cabron	slang for pig/imbecil – literally means goat
Hacienda	a large estate
Mayordomo	estate manager
Mucho gusto	a pleasure to meet you
Museo	museum
Semana Santa	Holy Week
Vaquero	cowboy
Venganza	revenge

Chapter 21

Bacalao	salted cod
Ceviche	raw fish marinated in lemon
Chilaquiles	traditional Mexican snack made from tortillas, shredded chicken and green tomato sauce
Cocina Mexicana	Mexican cuisine
Flautas	deep fried tacos stuffed with lettuce, cheese and chicken
Huevos	eggs/slang term for testicles
Gorditas	sweet, fluffy tortillas covered in shredded chicken, lettuce etc
Jicama	a yam or Mexican turnip
Mariscos	sea food
Mole	a turkey dish prepared in a rich chilli & chocolate sauce
Pulquerias	traditional bars/cantinas serving pulque, mezcal and Tequila
Salsa verde	green tomato and chilli sauce
Sopes	corn bread snack covered with meat and chilli sauce
Tapa	a snack, traditionally brought with an alcoholic drink in Spain

GLOSSARY

Chapter 22

Cabalgata	equestrian event/expedition
Curas	priests

Chapter 23

Cacique	tribal chief
Glorietta	roundabout
Periferico	orbital highway around Mexico City
Ponche	sweet punch
Posada	inn/Christmas festive procession

Chapter 24

Una carta	a letter
Zapatista	revolutionary party named after Emiliano Zapata

Chapter 25

Amigo	friend
Pinche	slang term for bloody/fucking
Taxis y taxistas	taxis and taxi drivers

Chapter 26

**La casa de
los espiritus**   house of spirits/haunted house

Chapter 27

Picaruelos   rogues/scoundrels/rascals

Chapter 29

**Casa de
Artesanias**   arts and crafts centre
Curandero   witch doctor
Jamaica   a drink made from hibiscus petals
Laguna Negra   hamlet in the vicinity of Vallle
Mal de ojo   evil eye
Micheladas   a beer based cocktail served with lemon, chilli & salt

Chapter 30

Huipil   traditional embroidered tunic for women
Jefe   chief/boss
La vida loca   living the wild life

GLOSSARY

Chapter 31

A Zihuatanejo	to Zihuatanejo
Agua de limon	lemonade
Altiplano	high mountain plateau/plain
El demonio	the demon/devil
El paso del infierno	hell's Pass
Huaraches	open sandals
Inocentes	the innocents
Mucho animo	wish you much luck
Palapa	a straw or thatched shelter

Chapter 32

Estrella	star/Girls' name
La muerte de Lupita Guadarama	the death of Lupita Guadarama
Marimba	Mexican xylophone
Paraiso	paradise
Playa de las gatas	beach of the cats/Cats' beach/beach in Zihuatanejo

Chapter 33

Cojones slang term for balls/testicles
El pinche gringo bloody foreigner

Chapter 34

Papel picado bunting made from tissue paper

Chapter 35

Abejas bees
El diente del Diablo the devil's teeth
El pescador fisherman
Turon an almond based confectionary

Chapter 37

El bocho the beetle/slang for VW Beetle
La carretera the road
Pension inn

Chapter 38

Las Aztecas The Aztecs

GLOSSARY

Los Campeones The Champions
La Copa
Mundial The World Cup
Los Ganadores The Winners

Chapter 39

Amigos
y conocidos friends and aquaintances
Bacalao salted cod
Hombres men
Lancha speed boat

Chapter 40

Perros Salvajes wild dogs

Chapter 41

Ayuntamiento town hall

Epilogue

Casa de
huespedes inn/hotel
Cicadas crickets
Narcos drug traffickers

ACKNOWLEDGEMENTS

I would like to thank the following people. Without their help, guidance, assistance and support this book would never have been written: Sharon, Keith Freeman, Andrew Dalton, Fiona Dunlop, Mark Carter, Julia Letts, Fidelma Feeney, Maria Naylor, Clare House, David & Helen George, Hilary Bower and Karen Fuller.